If we stay faithful in the middle of the story…

VICTORIOUS

…at the end of the story, we win.

MATT PROCTOR

A DEVOTIONAL STUDY OF
REVELATION

with small group
discussion questions

To my wife Katie,

*Like Revelation, you are an unfathomable mystery,
a beautiful vision and a blessing to my soul.*

Copyright © 2013 by College Press Publishing Company

Order at 800-289-3300 or on the web at www.collegepress.com

Cover and Book Design by Mandie Tepe

ISBN 978-0-89900-564-5

CONTENTS

Acknowledgments

I want to express thanks to my co-workers at Ozark Christian College who helped this book get to print—specifically Dru Ashwell, Kathy Bowers, and Greg Hafer—as well as to the OCC Trustee Board for their generous contribution that provided copies to the attendees at the 2013 North American Christian Convention.

I also want to acknowledge the help I found in several fine studies on Revelation—most notably those by my professor and friend Robert Lowery, Bruce Metzger, Mark Moore, Leon Morris, Robert Mounce, Eugene Peterson, and Scotty Smith. While any of this book's deficiencies are mine, any benefit here is because they taught me how to read Revelation.

INTRODUCTION

"Revelation was not written to promote speculation
but to produce determination."
— Rick Atchley —

Congratulations. You are a brave soul.

You just picked up a book on Revelation, and that took some courage. Revelation can be intimidating, and I know a lot of Christians who avoid it. Many believers have, in essence, only 65 books in their Bible because they never crack open the last one.

Of course, there are always a few folks infatuated with Revelation — the only book in their canon! But I'm going to assume that you feel a little trepidation about studying "the Apocalypse." That's to be expected: it's a challenging book to read, and more than one argument has started over its interpretation.

Tourists vs. Archaeologists

So let me take a few moments to let you know what to expect — and what not to expect — in the pages ahead. This book is NOT a commentary on Revelation, at least not in the traditional sense. I'm not going to explain every verse, and I'm not going to get super technical.

Although I've had the opportunity to study under one of the world's finest Revelation scholars, you won't find me exploring all the theological fine points or quoting lots of Greek words. (I once had a preaching professor who said that Greek in a sermon should be like underwear: it should provide good support but you shouldn't let it show!) Instead, I'll simply do my best to be understandable, readable, and faithful to the text.

For many of you, this is your first trip into the strange land of Revelation, so we're going to approach it less like an archaeologist and more like a tourist. An archaeologist sets up camp on a piece of geography for a long period of time, digs deep and seeks to unearth every hidden treasure available. A tourist, on the other hand, travels through the same territory in a shorter time frame, visits the landmarks and is just trying to get a first-time feel for the lay of the land.

That's what we'll do on our journey through this book. We'll survey the landscape, pick out the big themes, and give you a feel for these 22 chapters at the end of your Bible. On another day, I hope you'll return to stay longer and look closer, and there are great Revelation commentaries available to help you do an archaeologist's work, carefully examining all the details.

But in this brief study, my goal is just to be a good tour guide. In the first three chapters, I'll give some pre-trip instructions—important reminders to help you understand what you're seeing as we travel. In the remaining chapters, we'll trek through the book itself, picking out eight major themes as we do. I strongly recommend that you keep your Bible in hand, reading the chapters in Revelation that correspond to each chapter of this little book.

Rubik's Cube vs. Rescue Gear

As you read, you'll notice this study guide has a strong applicational focus. That's by design. Our driving question is not: "What can Revelation tell me about end time dates and details?" Instead, our question is: "What can Revelation tell me about being a faithful follower of Jesus?"

While Revelation certainly discusses the future, its primary purpose is not to reveal secret dates on a calendar, but to revive struggling disciples of Christ. As we'll soon see, this book was written to a group of first-century believers under siege. In the Roman Empire, they were a persecuted minority, a little band of soldiers surrounded by hostile forces. When you make an air drop to your troops trapped behind enemy lines, you don't send crossword puzzles. You send survival supplies—food and maps and tools to help get them out alive.

That's what the apostle John is doing in Revelation. The book is not intended to be a Rubik's Cube, a "last days puzzle" to solve. The book is meant to be rescue gear, equipment and instructions to get us safely home. Its purpose is practical, and so that will be our approach in this study.

Since "all Scripture is God-breathed and useful for . . . training in righteousness," we'll keep asking how Revelation trains us to be more righteous followers of Christ—people of greater faithfulness, stronger hope and deeper love (2 Tim 3:16). At the book's end, I've included questions for each chapter that, whether you're in a small group or on your own, will help you think through how God's message in Revelation applies to your life.

Thanks again for your courage in picking up this book. I think you'll find it was a life-changing decision.

CHAPTER ONE
THIS BOOK IS FOR YOU

*"Ten years ago our world had Bob Hope, Johnny Cash, and
Steve Jobs; now we have no Jobs, no Cash, and no Hope."*
— John Ortberg —

Have you ever felt hopeless?

May 23, 1939. In a world on the brink of war, the U.S. Navy was testing its newest submarine, the USS *Squalus*, off the coast of New Hampshire. Halfway through a training dive, a valve suddenly malfunctioned, and seawater began pouring into the submerged sub. Sirens sounded as the crew scrambled to seal off the flooding chambers, but not before 26 crewmen drowned. Now half-filled with water, the crippled submarine sank to the ocean floor.

Is There Any Hope?

With no power, the 33 remaining crew found themselves sitting in the dark in the forward sections of the *Squalus*, 243 feet below the surface. The temperature inside the sub began to drop rapidly in the near freezing water, and oxygen levels started to fall, creating increasingly toxic air. The situation was grim, and the men knew their survival time was measured in hours, not days.

These experienced submariners knew that a rescue was unlikely. Only a few years previous, another U.S. submarine sank off the Atlantic Coast, trapping six surviving crewmen. Navy divers had reached that downed sub, tapping on the hull in Morse code. One diver with his helmeted ear to the vessel heard the men inside tap back, "Is . . . there . . . any . . . hope?"

Sadly, despite the Navy's heroic efforts, the answer was no. All six surviving crewmen in that sub perished, and now as the *Squalus'* 33 surviving crewmen sat captive in the frigid dark, underneath the ocean's crushing pressure, they surely remembered that story. I imagine they asked themselves that same question, "Is there any hope?" Hearing nothing from the outside world for over seven hours, they suspected the answer was "no."

Help Is On the Way

But surprisingly, the answer was "yes." When fleet command could not hail the *Squalus*, a nearby submarine was ordered to search for her. When they located the *Squalus*, the sister-submarine crew banged on their hull in Morse code a message to the fallen sub, "Help ... is ... on ... the ... way." A rescuer was coming, but until he could arrive, they were given clear instructions for the meantime: "Remain calm. Stay quiet to conserve oxygen. Keep dry as possible."

Back at naval headquarters, USN Lieutenant Commander Charles Momsen had been developing a submarine rescue technology—a pressurized diving bell lowered on a huge winch to a submarine's escape hatch, allowing an airtight transfer of nine men from the sunken sub to the surface. Now his new device would be put to the test. As soon as he received word about the *Squalus*, Momsen flew from Washington, D.C. to New Hampshire, boarded the rescue ship *USS Falcon*, and immediately began directing the rescue efforts.

Amazingly—despite rough weather, near-zero visibility, jammed cables and the ticking clock—Momsen was able to lower the diving bell four times over the course of thirteen hours, and all 33 men were saved. When the last survivor stepped onto the deck of the *Falcon*, Charles Momsen's watch read 12:38 a.m., May 25th. It had been 39 hours since the *Squalus* sank.

The rescue has been called "the navy's most successful failure." Victory had been seized from the brink of defeat, and Momsen was awarded a presidential commendation. In a hopeless situation, a hero had appeared.

When You Feel Trapped In the Dark

Hopeless. Maybe you've been there—at the very brink of defeat, under-neath the world's pressures, trapped in a crushing situation:

- You've just returned from the cemetery where you buried your husband, and the silent house threatens to overwhelm you with grief.
- You're struggling with a dark temptation, and every time you lose a battle, the guilt gnaws at your soul.
- You wake up with the lingering aftertaste of last night's argument. Your marriage is in shambles, and you don't know what to do.

- You took a stand at work . . . and lost your job. You kept your integrity, but your stack of bills is getting higher as your bank account gets lower.
- You've poured prayer and sweat into a new ministry, but nothing's happening. You thought you were called, but now you're wracked with doubt.

Let's face it: life is hard, and the Christian life is harder. We try to follow Jesus, but we discover that the road is paved with pain. Faith is not a force field, and believers aren't protected from all of life's dangers. In a fallen world, we still experience car wrecks and cancer, and as followers of Jesus, we're actually promised more trials. The apostle Paul wrote, "Everyone who wants to live a godly life in Christ Jesus will be persecuted" (2 Tim 3:12). Peter reminds us, "Do not be surprised at the fiery ordeal that has come on you" (1 Pet 4:12). Jesus himself said, "In this world you will have trouble" (John 16:33).

Sometimes in the midst of those troubles, it can seem like all hope is lost.

My friend Becky has dealt with more than her share of tragedy. Several years ago her father died in a plane crash. She has a brother who's strung out on drugs. But Becky's other brother was the bright spot in the family—a strapping young man, U. S. Marine, big smile, bigger heart. Then came the day he was killed in a car accident.

My wife and I drove three hours to the funeral visitation. I'll never forget the date—September 11, 2001—and when we arrived at the funeral home, I walked up beside Becky, put my arm around her and said, "We are so sorry." She turned to me, and in language too raw for me to use here, she whispered through clenched teeth, "Matt, I am so hacked off at God."

She was there: trapped alone in the dark, gasping for oxygen beneath an ocean of pain, certain that God had forgotten her. Behind her angry words, I could hear her heart's despairing cry, "Is . . . there . . . any . . . hope?"

The Most Dangerous Place In the World

That was surely the cry of the believers in Asia Minor. In the final years of the first century, the emperor Domitian ruled the Roman Empire with an iron fist. A brutally powerful dictator, Domitian was so hated that, upon his death, the Roman Senate immediately passed a *damnatio memoriae*, an official damnation of his memory. His coins and statues were melted, his architectural projects were torn down and his name was erased from all public records. During his 15-year reign, Domitian demonstrated ruthless efficiency in eliminating threats—even executing 20 senators who opposed him, including three of his own family members.

Unfortunately, Domitian saw Christians as a threat. Deeply committed to the Roman religious pantheon, he not only enforced the worship of the Roman gods, but he also instituted the worship of himself as a god, a practice called the *imperial cult*. Citizens of the empire paid homage to his statues and called Domitian by the title *Dominus et Deus*, which means "Lord and God."

When Christians refused to worship the Roman deities, Domitian charged them, ironically, with atheism—they didn't believe in the gods. When the first-century believers would not pay homage to his statue and instead called Jesus "Lord and God," Domitian saw this as an act of treason. Clearly, they were pledging allegiance to another King. So while Christians had been sporadically persecuted before, under Domitian the persecution of Christians became official empire policy.

If you followed Jesus, you were suddenly at the top of the Empire's hit list. The Roman version of the FBI could harass you, arrest you, even execute you. To a Christian, Rome became the most dangerous place in the world. So the believers went underground—literally. They began to dig catacombs beneath the city where they could secretly meet to worship and to bury their dead, hiding in fear of Roman retribution.

If anyone felt trapped in the dark, underneath crushing circumstances, it was those early Christians. You can almost hear a whisper echoing in those subterranean tombs: "Is...there...any...hope?"

They needed a *hero* to appear.

The Easy Chair Is Just As Dangerous

So near the end of the first century—around 95 A.D., the apostle John picked up his pen to write the believers in seven cities in the Roman Empire. These cities, located on one long mail route through the province of Asia Minor, were each home to a church, many of which were under fire. The saints in Ephesus had endured hardships for Christ's name (Rev 2:3). Those in Smyrna had been slandered and would be put in prison (Rev 2:9-10). In Pergamum, Antipas had already been killed (Rev 2:13). These are "not minor daily trials or inconvenient obstacles. The first-century believers to whom Revelation was addressed were facing martyrdom, not flat tires."[1] They were in deep despair.

So John writes to challenge them with one simple message: *stay faithful to Jesus*.

As a wise pastor, John knows these believers are facing two threats. On the one hand is the threat of outright persecution. Confronted with the possibility of losing their jobs, their freedom and even their lives, these Christians might decide it's easier to turn their backs on Jesus. "Forget Christianity. I don't want to get arrested. Let's just go back to the old ways—worshipping Jupiter never got anybody killed."

On the other hand, John knows, is a second and greater threat: cultural seduction. Because of the persecution, the early Christians will be tempted to blend in with their surroundings—to conform to the values and lifestyles of the culture around them. The Enemy doesn't have to destroy the believers through open conflict; he will simply dilute them through subtle compromise. They don't want to draw attention to themselves, so get them comfortable with the moral standards of their Roman next-door neighbors. Why push them into the electric chair when the easy chair will do? If they will just relax their obedience a bit to "fit in," then the devil's job is done. They will be "lukewarm—neither hot nor cold" and God will spit them out of His mouth (3:16).

John's Life Is a Sermon Too

To those facing both physical persecution and cultural seduction, John's message rings out: *stay faithful to Jesus*. John writes Revelation to challenge his readers not to give in to the world. This book is not a crystal ball but a megaphone—a trumpet call to loyalty and endurance and radical holiness of life.

By the way, John knows something about faithfulness under fire. He has experienced plenty of persecution himself. In Acts, he and Peter were arrested multiple times for preaching the gospel. (John is

---

1. Mike Graves, *The Sermon as Symphony* (Valley Forge: Judson Press, 1997) 244-245.

what we could call a "repeat offender.") They are even flogged (Acts 5:40). If you've seen the movie *The Passion of the Christ*, you know the horror of a flogging, and John's body bore the scars of his commitment to Christ.

Yet, John never faltered. Even now, as he writes Revelation as an 80-something-year-old man, the aged apostle finds himself imprisoned one last time. John is exiled on the island of Patmos in the Aegean Sea. This barren rock, 37 miles from the mainland, was the Roman Alcatraz. He has been sentenced there for proclaiming "the word of God and the testimony of Jesus," and he will never leave (Rev 1:9). Nobody escaped from Patmos. But John does not despair. Instead, he writes with power and conviction and trust.

His life is preaching the same sermon that his book does: *stay faithful to Jesus.*

Lucky Charms and the Contemporary Church

So if you have ever been tempted to compromise your faith even a little — to conform to the surrounding culture — this book is for you.

My favorite cereal is Lucky Charms. I personally believe that Lucky Charms are evidence of a good God. My wife, however, is not so charmed with my cereal choice . . . because of the price. She is frugal and stretches every dollar in our family budget. I'm not making this up: she used to subscribe to a magazine called *Cheapskate Monthly,* filled with money-saving ideas. There is actually another magazine called the *Tightwad Gazette,* but we didn't subscribe to it. (Too much money.)

So when we first went grocery shopping together after we got married, Katie was aghast to discover how expensive Lucky Charms were: "Look at the unit price, Matt! Surely this generic brand over here would be just as good." I explained to her that nothing could compete with the marshmallowy goodness of Lucky Charms, and I put the big red box in our shopping cart.

A few weeks later, I stumbled bleary-eyed into the kitchen one Saturday morning, grabbed my big red box of Lucky Charms, and poured them in my bowl with some milk. But after the first bite, I knew that something was terribly wrong. Do you know what my wife had done? She had bought a box of generic "Magic Stars" and put them in my Lucky Charms box! She thought I would never know the difference.

They were not magically delicious.

The outside packaging looked genuine, but the inside contents were a cheap imitation. Too often, that can be a description of my life. I can look like a real Christian to all observers: go to church, sing the songs, pray the prayers, read my Bible and even give my money. But if I'm honest, I'm not always living the life. I can watch the same boundary-pushing TV shows as my non-Christian neighbors, listen to the same music, use the same swear words, share the same gossip, follow the same selfish spending patterns, and think the same world-tainted thoughts.

I'm not the only one who has fallen prey to Satan's subtle compromises. To the believers at Sardis, Jesus said, "I know your deeds; you have a reputation of being alive, but you are dead" (3:1). Their outside packaging looked genuine, but the inside contents were a cheap imitation.

By the way, Jesus might say the same to the American church. Ronald Sider's book, *The Scandal of the Evangelical Conscience: Why Christians Are Living Just Like the Rest of the World*, cites surveys showing that American Christians aren't living much differently than our culture—percentages of spousal abuse, giving habits, cohabitation, divorce, racism and addiction to pornography are almost the same as those among non-Christians.[2] Despite the appearance of commitment, the contemporary church is plagued by shallow faith.

Revelation is just the book we need to call us deeper—to true faithfulness to Christ.

This Book Is For You

But it's not just a call to holiness. At the end of the day, Revelation is a call to hope. Maybe you're not facing physical persecution like those early believers. But maybe you do find yourself on the brink of defeat, crushed under an ocean of pain, sitting alone in the dark. This book is for you.

When you feel trapped in hopeless circumstances, Revelation is

---

2. Ronald Sider, *The Scandal of the Evangelical Conscience: Why Christians Are Living Just Like the Rest of the World* (Grand Rapids: Baker Books, 2005) 13.

Morse code, tapping out a message, "Help . . . is . . . on . . . the . . . way." Stay faithful, says John, because a **hero** is coming.

Until our rescuer arrives, Revelation gives clear instructions for the meantime, and in the pages ahead, we'll explore those instructions. This study guide focuses on Jesus' instructions for us while we wait—things like loving the church honestly (chapter 5), enduring suffering patiently (chapter 7), bearing witness boldly (chapter 8), and seeing evil clearly (chapter 9). Revelation teaches us how to hang on until help arrives.

But most of all, Revelation tells us that a day is coming when we will be rescued. A Savior will enter our world again (19:11). This time, he will come not as a baby, but as a warrior. Not humbly on a donkey, but triumphantly on a warhorse. Not to be delivered to his enemies, but to deliver us from our enemies. He will come with power, majesty, might and authority—to set us free from captivity, to release us from our circumstances and to take us back to a brighter, better world. He will snatch us from the edge of defeat and lead us into victory. What a day that will be! This is the message of Revelation: *If we stay faithful in the middle of the story, we will be victorious in the end.*

That is good news, and the believers in Asia Minor needed that message. The book of Revelation shot the spiritual adrenaline of hope through their weary souls.

You need it too. You need the book of Revelation. As we work together through this study, you will feel fresh strength surge through your spiritual muscles. You will sense new life coursing through your veins. You will begin to walk in victorious confidence, even in the valley of the shadow of death, because you will know how the story ends.

"Is . . . there . . . any . . . hope?"

The answer is yes. A hero is coming. Help is on the way.

Disscussion Questions
Chapter 1
This Book Is For You

1. Describe a time when you felt hopeless or in need of rescue. How did that feel?

2. Have you experienced hositility because of your faith? In what ways does this happen in our culture?

3. How might the American church be tempted to conform to our culture? What happens when we compromise?

4. What kind of message would encourage a discouraged church? What do you think will help us stay faithful to Jesus over the long haul?

CHAPTER TWO
IT'S NOT AS HARD
AS YOU THINK

*"The book to read is not the one which thinks for you,
but the one which makes you think.
No book in the world equals the Bible for that."*
— Harper Lee —

When I interviewed for my first preaching ministry at age 23, I told the search committee that I believed in the power of God's Word. I told them I was convinced that "all Scripture is God-breathed and is useful for teaching, rebuking, correcting and training in righteousness" (2 Tim 3:16). I affirmed my commitment to proclaim "the whole counsel of God" (Acts 20:27).

That wasn't 100% true.

That commitment was 65/66 true, but at that point in my life, there was one book of the Bible I didn't preach, one part of "all Scripture" that I avoided, one portion of "the whole counsel of God" that I didn't even read.

The book of Revelation.

Staying Away From the Haunted House

Revelation just didn't seem "useful," and as a young Christian, I steered clear of the last book of the Bible. I wasn't the only one. "I don't think I really *need* to read Revelation," said a woman in my church. "It doesn't make any sense, and the rest of the Bible already tells me what I need to know."

Fred Craddock says that reading through the New Testament is like walking down the street. The Gospels are first, and they are well-lit, a familiar neighborhood. Next comes Paul, still friendly territory, but as you move through the epistles, the shadows grow deeper, the houses more neglected, until suddenly you see it. There at the end of the street, shrouded in darkness, stands the frightening, haunted house of Revelation.[1]

---

1. Fred Craddock, "Reflections on an Early Christian Sermon: Form," *Abilene Christian University Lectures on Preaching* (Abilene: 1999).

Not many Christians want to go in there.

The reasons for staying out of Revelation are many. First of all, *the book is just flat hard to understand.* The church father Jerome said, "Revelation has as many mysteries as it does words." Martin Luther said the book of Revelation ought to be kicked out of the Bible because it doesn't *reveal* anything. Let's face it: bizarre images of strange creatures, a beast with ten horns and claws of bronze, stars falling from the heavens, a great red dragon with seven heads, 666, blood, bowls of sulfur, people eating scrolls, bottomless pits, dragons, the four horses of the Apocalypse, war, pestilence, famine and death aren't normal water cooler conversation. This is strange stuff, and as someone put it, "Revelation doesn't seem like a very *happy* book." As a young preacher, I couldn't make heads or tails of it, so I just stayed away.

Another reason believers sometimes ignore Revelation is because *it's been so abused.* No other book in the Bible has sparked more obsession, strange teaching and wild speculation than Revelation. When I started Bible college in the fall of 1988, everyone on campus was talking about Edgar Whisenant's book *88 Reasons Why Jesus Will Come Again in 1988* which predicted Jesus' return in mid-September. (Matthew 24:36 says we can't know the day or the hour, but apparently we can know the month and the year!) Of course, he was wrong.

I read about another preacher who claimed that "the literal building blocks for the new temple in Israel have been constructed and numbered and are being stored in the basements of K-Marts all over the United States until they can be shipped to Israel and used to build a new temple."[2] (Seriously? K-Mart? If there's a new world order coming, everyone knows it's going to come from Wal-Mart.)

Revelation seems to attract wild-eyed, delusional characters, prompting G. K. Chesterton to remark that "though St. John saw many strange monsters in his vision, he saw no creature so wild as one of his own commentators." I certainly didn't want to be lumped in with those guys. To avoid guilt by association, I avoided Revelation.

As a young minister, one final reason I stayed away from Revelation was what I'll call *job security.* I liked being employed, and

---

2. John Ortberg, *Experience God's Power* (Grand Rapids: Zondervan, 2002) 12.

if this book was so controversial and divisive, why should I stir up trouble? After all, I heard the true story of a preacher in Ohio who was teaching on Revelation, and when he finished, somebody shot him. I thought, "I'm 23 years old. I'm too young to die. I'll just stick with the Psalms."

Time To Teach Revelation

But a turning point came for me during that first ministry. I was enrolled in seminary and signed up for a class on Revelation by Dr. Robert Lowery, a world-class scholar on the book. In those sixteen weeks, my eyes were opened. Dr. Lowery immersed me in the faith-shaping images of this book. As he taught us how to read Revelation, I was swept up in the epic vision—the cosmic battle raging between Lamb and Dragon, a battle waged in the earthbound lives of first century believers, a battle for the allegiance and eternal destiny of human hearts and minds.

I learned that I needed Revelation. I also began to see that my church needed Revelation.

After all, it *is* part of "all Scripture," it *is* "God-breathed," it *is* "useful for teaching," and it *is* part of "the whole counsel of God." It is a significant portion of divine revelation, it is the culmination of the Old and New Testaments, and it answers the essential human question of what this world is coming to.

When David Buttrick was growing up, his family's guest room was always filled. He tells the story of a time the children played a practical joke:

> They sneaked into the guest room, took the mystery novel off the bedside table, tore out the last chapter, and returned the book to its place. The next morning, the guest came to the breakfast table bleary-eyed and curious. What happened in the last chapter? How did it turn out? He went home, found the mystery in a second-hand bookstore, and finished it. To his great surprise, some things he thought were important turned out to be irrelevant and some things he had ignored became most important in the end.[3]

3. H. Stephen Shoemaker, *GodStories* (Valley Forge: Judson Press, 1998) 304.

Revelation tells how the story of God's people ends, and only when our people know the end of their story can they make sense of the story's middle where they live right now.

My people needed to read Revelation.

I also began to realize: A preacher's job is not just to teach his congregation God's Word. It is also to teach them how to read God's Word for themselves. If this is true for the first 65 books of the Bible, it is truest of the 66th book. So, I would need to give my people a few interpretive tools to help them read Revelation correctly—to pass along what Dr. Lowery had taught me. I focused on teaching three interpretive keys: the literary style, the symbols and the structure of Revelation.

With these three keys in your hand, unlocking Revelation's message is not as hard as you think. I'll talk about the first key in this chapter, and the remaining two keys in the next chapter.

THE STYLE OF REVELATION

Another Time and Another Place

First, I knew that my congregation needed to understand the apocalyptic style of Revelation. Apocalypse was a type of literature familiar to ancient readers. Some Old Testament prophets—Isaiah, Ezekiel, Daniel—included apocalyptic sections in their messages, and other non-canonical apocalypses were floating around as well.

What exactly is an apocalypse? The word itself means an "unveiling," and the purpose of apocalyptic literature is "to interpret present, earthly circumstances in light of the supernatural world and of the future, and to influence both the understanding and the behavior of the audience."[4] In other words, a vision of another time and another place was intended to shape how you lived in this time and this place.

A contemporary example: I was eight years old when *Star Wars* first hit theaters, and I was immediately swept up into a "galaxy far, far away" with Luke Skywalker and the rag-tag Rebel Alliance as they took on Darth Vader and the evil Empire. (I may or may not have named my oldest son Luke just so I could say in my deepest voice, "Luke, I am your father.")

---

4. Adela Yarbro Collins, "Introduction: Early Christian Apocalypticism" *Semeia* 36 (1986) 7.

Mark Wegierski notes:

> The *Star Wars* movies arrived at a critical time in American history. Post-Vietnam malaise, the oil crisis and an economic recession—as well as the feeling that "there was nothing right with America"—had characterized the 1970s. The *Star Wars* trilogy clearly served as a fresh tonic, rekindling the breezy optimism in the American psyche.[5]

During this time, President Reagan sought popular support for his strategy to win the Cold War with the Soviet Union. In a 1983 speech, he famously characterized the Soviet Union as an "evil empire." While media critics chastised such language, many Americans immediately identified with the allusion. The "monochromatic, militaristic Galactic Empire" in *Star Wars* looked a lot like the Soviet Union.

Besides, what American wouldn't want to imagine himself as part of the scrappy, democratic, multicultural Rebel Alliance fighting against the odds for freedom against tyranny?[6] Reagan captured the national imagination by applying a futuristic, otherworldly image to a present-day, this-worldly reality. We saw our world in terms of that other world.

That's what apocalyptic literature does. It addresses our contemporary "thoughts, attitudes, and feelings by the use of effective symbols and a narrative plot that invites imaginative participation."[7] John's narrative of dragons and angels and swords is not just a story of some future time, but is meant to be the story of our time. His readers are meant to be swept up into the drama, imagining themselves as participants in the cosmic struggle of which he writes.

That Story Is My Story

When the *Lord of the Rings* movies were released shortly after the 9-11 tragedy, Americans resonated with the epic. It was an unironic story of good versus evil, courage, friendship, the defense of an idyllic way of life under siege by an unfathomable and formless enemy, and the need to create a multilateral fellowship for the common good. In those days after the Twin Towers fell, we as viewers somehow felt that Tolkien's story wasn't about Middle-Earth. It was about us. That was our story.

---

5. Mark Wegierski, "Reagan: Jedi Knight" *World* (May 22, 1999).
6. *Ibid.*
7. Adela Yarbro Collins, *Crisis and Catharsis: The Power of the Apocalypse* (Philadelphia: Westminster, 1984) 145.

That was the experience of John's readers. They realized that his world of huge harlots and terrible beasts was really their own Roman world of bustling marketplaces and cheering Coliseums . . . and if we read carefully, we will realize that it's our world of minivans and Super Bowls and shopping malls. In apocalypse, no matter how strange the tale, we are meant to see that it is our story.

So apocalyptic style envisions a strange world in order to recast the way we see our familiar world. All of which means: *if Revelation is our story, then we are living in a cosmic narrative of epic proportions.*

We, too, often suppose that our lives are utterly ordinary. We get up every day at the same time, drive the same car to the same job, and come home to the same supper table. We mow the same yard, watch the same TV show, kiss the same spouse, go to sleep in the same bed, and wake up tomorrow morning to do it all over again. To the outside observer, and even to our own eyes, our lives look respectably boring and largely unremarkable. The devil wants to lull us into thinking that what we see is all that's going on.

But Revelation throws back the curtain on the spiritual world all around us — a world inhabited by angels and demons, a cosmos roiling in spiritual battle, an enemy at work insidiously influencing the culture around us, and a historical timeline bending toward a crisis of universal proportions — a judgment day when the eternal destiny of every human soul will be finally and fully decided. Your little daily routines are *not* all that is going on. Revelation tells us that we are players in the drama of the ages.

You may be saying, "That's the world in which I live?! I thought my story was much more . . . mundane. I had no idea!"

You're Part Of an Epic Tale

That's the purpose of Revelation's unique literary style. John's apocalypse "rips the veneer of cliché off everyday routines and reveals the side-by-side splendors and terrors of heaven and hell. Apocalypse is arson — it secretly sets a fire in the imagination" that burns away the enemy's façade, dissolves the "virtual reality" he seeks to create, and exposes reality in all its stark-but-hopeful clarity.[8]

When we read Revelation, we suddenly realize that, "with the vastness of the heavenly invasion and the urgency of the faith decision

---

8. Eugene Peterson, *The Contemplative Pastor* (Dallas: Word Publishing, 1989) 51.

rolling into our consciousness like thunder and lightning, we cannot stand around on Sunday morning filling our time with pretentious small talk."[9] We are part of something bigger than that.

I knew a Bible college professor once—a self-proclaimed nerd—who would play the *Star Wars* theme music every morning as he shaved. (He was an apologetics professor who told his students he was training them to be "Apolojedi.") This professor said that John Williams' grand, sweeping score reminded him that he was not simply getting ready to go give a few lectures, grade a few papers, talk to a few students and then come home. No. That music reminded him that he was preparing to play his part in the cosmic battle of good versus evil, that the stakes were high, that the story in which he was living was epic and that—even in all the small decisions he made that day—he must fight courageously and never let down his guard.

That's what apocalypse does, and that's why as a young preacher, I finally decided to preach Revelation. I needed the reminder that my story was larger-than-this-life, and so did my people.

Maybe you do too. With Dr. Lowery's three interpretive keys, you'll dis-cover that reading Revelation is not as hard as you think. In the next chapter, we'll look at the other two interpretive keys—Revelation's symbols and its structure. But for now, hear the message of its apocalyptic style.

You're part of something big.

---

9. *Ibid.*, 47.

DISSCUSSION QUESTIONS
Chapter 2
It's Not As Hard As You Think

1. Name a time Scripture has encouraged you, challenged you or equipped you.

2. What fears do you have about studying Revelation? What are some good reasons to study it?

3. Have you ever thought of your life as utterly ordinary? How would it change your life if you discovered you were part of an epic story?

4. What possibiities excit you about this study? What kind of "teaching, rebuking, correctin and training in righteousness" might God want to do in your life (2 Tim 3:36)?

CHAPTER THREE
YOU WILL BE BLESSED

*"A Bible that is falling apart usually
belongs to someone who isn't."*
—Charles Spurgeon—

In a Revelation sermon series at Chicago's Willow Creek Community Church, pastor John Ortberg wanted to teach his listeners to interpret the book's symbols as the original readers wouldhave. He asked them to imagine reading the following paragraph on the sports page of the Chicago Tribune in the winter of 1999.

"The bull which once ruled the earth for 72 months has suffered a mighty fall. For at the end of the 72 months, the great right horn of the bull—whose number is twenty and three (let the reader understand)—departed, and so did the great left horn of the bull. Then the third horn of the bull, which was pierced in many places and dressed like a woman, likewise departed. Then all the beasts of the earth—the hornets and timberwolves—came and devoured the flesh of the bull, and the glory of the mighty bull was laid low."

Can you guess what sport that paragraph is describing? If you lived in Chicago in the winter of 1999, you would know the sport the writer was talking about was ... basketball, of course.[1]

THE SYMBOLS OF REVELATION

As a young preacher, I knew the second interpretive key my people needed was an understanding of Revelation's symbolism. John is a poet, and in an attempt to convey the incredible vision he is given, John ransacks the Greek language for all the metaphors he can find. He pillages the Old Testament for images—over 500 Old Testament

---

1. For those who don't follow sports, or just slept through the '90s, let me briefly explain. After the great Michael Jordan, jersey number 23, retired from the NBA Champion Chicago Bulls, the team's two other key players—Scottie Pippen and the heavily pierced, cross-dressing Dennis Rodman—also left. The once great Bulls were suddenly getting beaten by mediocre teams like the Charlotte Hornets and Minnesota Timberwolves.

allusions in 404 verses—as he pushes language to the breaking point trying to capture what he's seeing. Numbers, colors, animals, objects and geographical places are all used to convey larger realities.

But these images can be hard to understand. Two thousand years from now, the above paragraph from the *Chicago Tribune* sports page would seem unintelligible to a future reader, because they wouldn't know the historical background of the symbolic language.

Or how about this: If an African picked up today's American newspaper, he might see on the editorial page a cartoon of an elephant and donkey playing tug-o-war. As cultural insiders, we immediately understand the political reference, but our African friend might think that Americans train their animals for some strange contests. When we pick up Revelation with its pictures of bizarre beasts and two-thousand-year-old references, we can feel the same confusion, because we are cultural outsiders to the first-century Graeco-Roman world.

What's the History Behind the Image?

So to understand Revelation's symbolism, the first question we'll want to ask is: what are the historical associations of the symbol? Rather than reading twenty-first century connections into the text, my seminary professor Dr. Lowery taught us to look for the first-century connections.

Some teachers today who read about great flying locusts with breastplates like iron, wings that sound like thundering horses and the sting of scorpions in their tails see that as a reference to modern-day Apache helicopters flying through John's apocalypse (Rev 9:9-10). But a better approach is to ask what John's first readers would have understood. Answer: probably not helicopters. (You can read more in chapter 8 about what they probably understood.) Keep Revelation's metaphors in their historical context.

Another brief example: In John's description of the new heavens and the new earth, he says "there was no longer any sea" (Rev 21:1). At first blush, we might think that's unfortunate. No sea in heaven? "Sea" is a warm word in my dictionary. My family loves the Florida beach! Is John saying we will no longer watch in awe as the ocean waves crash on Oregon's rocky coast?

To understand John's imagery, however, you'll need to put on your first-century sandals. To the ancients, the sea was a symbol of chaos and evil. "The wicked are like the tossing sea, which cannot rest, whose waves cast up mire and mud" (Isa 57:20). The sea divided people from loved ones over seemingly uncrossable distances, brought storms and invading enemies, and even vomited forth the wicked beast himself (Rev 13:1).

When we understand "sea" was a terrifying word in the first-century dictionary, we will realize that John is not making a geographical statement, but a theological one. When John says it, his first-century readers felt their hearts lift: no more sea meant no more danger, no more division, no more evil! To them, this was good news indeed.

But we only understand this if we put ourselves in their sandals. So as we read Revelation's symbols, we'll want to keep them against their historical background, and they will make much more sense.

What Feelings Does the Picture Produce?

The second question we'll want to ask: what are the emotional associations of the symbol? Certainly an American flag has particular factual references: thirteen stripes stand for thirteen original colonies, fifty stars stand for fifty states. But the Stars and Stripes also carry emotional connotations: bravery, sacrifice, freedom and home. The image of the Red, White and Blue can actually bring a lump to someone's throat. Metaphors are pictures that don't just convey content; they conjure powerful feelings. While a symbol has an objective referent, it also has an emotional pulse.

So how about the images of Revelation? What emotions do they evoke? Don't make this harder than it is: a Lamb is innocent and vulnerable, a Lion is fierce and noble, and a Dragon is frighteningly large and evil. These images are meant to stir something in our hearts, but sometimes in our attempts to explain a symbol, some of its evocative power can be lost. Overexplaining can "unweave the rainbow."

For example, maybe the precious stones in the New Jerusalem's foundation each have a specific factual meaning (Rev 21:19-20). Jasper, sapphire, agate, emerald, onyx, ruby, chysolite, beryl, topaz, turquoise, jacinth, amethyst: maybe they are meant to convey twelve different and distinct truths about the city of God.

Or . . . maybe these varied precious gems are simply meant to create a dazzling vision of beauty and color and inestimable worth. Maybe we aren't meant to crack open our dictionary to find the historical associations of "onyx." Maybe instead, as we look at the New Jerusalem's foundation, we're simply intended to catch our breath, stand in wonder at the richness of the city that will one day be our home, and marvel at God's exquisite craftsmanship and creativity. As Bruce Metzger describes:

> This book contains a series of word pictures, as though a number of slides were being shown upon a great screen. As we watch we allow ourselves to be carried along by impressions created by these pictures. Many of the details of the pictures are intended to contribute to the total impression, and are not to be isolated and interpreted with wooden literalism.[2]

In other words, as my seminary professor Dr. Lowery taught us: don't overpress the details of the symbolism. Even a child can watch the images of Revelation and catch the story's basic plot: an evil dragon is attacking the bride of our hero, and she must stay faithful to him as she waits for the day when he rides back victoriously to take her to his castle.

That's not to say that understanding details doesn't matter, but as Leland Ryken reminds us:

> The truth is that for the most part the images and symbols of Revelation are universal . . . . Its images are those of our waking and sleeping dreams — lamb, dragon, beast, water, sea, sun, war, harvest, bride, throne, jewels. Its color symbolism is equally universal — light for goodness, darkness for evil, red for bloodshed and perverse passion. Heaven is high, as we have always known it to be, and hell is low and bottomless . . . . The book of Revelation does not require a guidebook to esoteric symbols. It requires a keen eye for the obvious.[3]

2. Bruce Metzger, *Breaking the Code: Understanding the Book of Revelation* (Nashville: Abingdon, 1993) 11.
3. Leland Ryken and Tremper Longman, eds. *A Complete Literary Guide to the Bible* (Grand Rapids: Zondervan, 1993) 460.

THE STRUCTURE OF REVELATION

As a young preacher, the final interpretive key I needed to give my churchfolk was an understanding of Revelation's structure. They needed a basic outline of Revelation so they could make sense of what they were reading – so they could get the big sweep of the book. One friend suggested a simple outline of Revelation:

1. Things Are Bad
2. Things Are Going to Get Worse
3. We Win

That's not bad for starters! But I wanted to keep pushing for more specific labels. So here was my attempt: chapters 1-3 might be *Jesus counsels the church*, while chapters 4-5 might be *Jesus controls the universe*, as we see the Lamb on the throne with the scroll of history in His hand. Chapters 6-11 with the seven seals and seven trumpets of judgment might be *Jesus condemns the earth*.

In chapters 12-20 the conflict deepens and moves from the earthly sphere into the heavenlies where Christ is ultimately victorious, so a label might be *Jesus conquers Satan*. The book climaxes with the New Jerusalem coming down out of heaven like a bride beautifully dressed for her husband, so chapters 21-22 might be *Jesus consummates his long-awaited marriage*.

Commentaries can give you an even more detailed structure to the book, but the point of any Revelation outline is simply this: in the midst of all the mind-blowing noise, visuals and special effects, there's a powerful story here – a discernible and understandable plot that drives the whole book. Don't miss it.

What Is Progressive Parallelism?

Before we wrap up this final interpretive key, I need to tackle one unique feature of Revelation's structure. It's a little tricky, but if you'll hang with me, I think it will make sense, and it will help you understand Revelation's flow better.

Because so much of Revelation deals with the three "sevens of judgments" – the seven seals (Rev 6-8), the seven trumpets (Rev 8-11) and the seven bowls (Rev 15-16) – I need to give some special attention to the structure of these sequences. A helpful concept for understanding their structure is "progressive parallelism."

Progressive parallelism is a form of writing which states a truth, then restates it in a more complete way. Example: "My daughter is fourteen; she is a teenager." In that sentence, the second half does not simply restate the truth of the first half, but advances the idea. Saying my daughter is fourteen tells you how old she is, but telling you she's a *teenager* carries a whole different level of meaning—suggesting a particular world of music, clothes, habits and hormones. (Parents, can I get an "Amen?") The second half of my sentence not only parallels the truth of the first half; it progresses it, fleshing it out more fully.

The apostle John was a good Jewish boy, and Jewish literature is packed with progressive parallelism. (The Psalms and Proverbs are loaded with it!) So did John incorporate progressive parallelism into the structure of Revelation? I believe he did.

A Unique Movie

I once saw a movie that used a fascinating storytelling device. Entitled Vantage Point, it was a political action thriller starring Dennis Quaid as a Secret Service agent who, in the opening 20 minutes of the movie witnesses the U.S. president get shot by an unknown assassin. Then the movie rewinds and you watch the same event – the presidential assination--unfold five more times, each time from the vantage point of a different character.

As the viewer, you're trying to discover—along with Quaid's character—who targeted the President. Each successive "rewind" provides more details, filling in the plot until the truth is finally known. The movie was a classic example of progressive parallelism in narrative form.

Many scholars believe that's exactly what the apostle John was using in the book of Revelation—specifically in the three "sevens of judgment": the seals, trumpets and bowls. In other words, these three sequences are not necessarily in chronological order like some 21-point timeline of events to come. They may not be describing three different chapters in world history—a chapter of seals, followed by a chapter of trumpets, followed by a chapter of bowls.

Rather, each of these three sequences is likely describing the same chapter of world history. That chapter is the time period from John's writing to Christ's return. Each "seven of judgment," then, narrates the world's sufferings that God uses through the ages to judge sin and prompt repentance, and each "seven of judgment" brings us to the same moment in time—the end of the world.

Like the movie *Vantage Point*, we are watching the same scenario unfold before us multiple times; instead of a presidential assassination, we're watching God's judgments ultimately leading up to the end of time. In each set of seven, we're simply seeing the same fateful chapter in history three different times.

"Once More From the Top, Only Louder"

But the three "sevens of judgment" are not simply parallel, repeating the same event. They exhibit *progressive* parallelism because in each successive sequence, God's judgment intensifies. In our first look at God's coming judgment (the seven seals), a fourth of the world is affected (Rev 6:8). In our second look (the seven trumpets), a third of the world is affected (Rev 8:7-12). In our final look (the seven bowls), no fractions are used — *all* of the world is affected (Rev 16:1-21).

Reading through the three sequences of judgment, you can almost picture God as a conductor who, after hearing his orchestra play a musical selection, wants them to run through the piece again with more intensity. After the first two judgment sequences, it's as if he lifts his conductor's baton and instructs his angels of judgment, "Once more from the top, only louder this time!"

Why would God show us the same event three times in the same book — each time a little louder? Quite simply, it's to drive the message home. An old Czech proverb says, "Repetition is the mother of wisdom," and as the Great Communicator, God often repeats himself in Scripture. He runs us through these catastrophic scenes in Revelation three times to reinforce his message: he will not let evil go unpunished — judgment is coming — so the people of the earth should make themselves ready.

One last thing: an interlude appears between the sixth and seventh of each judgment group. Between the sixth and seventh seals, Revelation 7:1-17 stresses the saints' *security*. In the seven trumpets, the interlude at Revelation 10:1-11:14 stresses the saints' *witness*. In the seven bowls, the brief interlude at Revelation 16:15 stresses the saints' *vigilance*.[4] By repeating the sequence three times, God reminds his people of three different responses to the coming judgment: they should trust his protection, proclaim his truth, and keep themselves prepared.

---

4. See Robert Lowery, *Revelation's Rhapsody* (Joplin: College Press, 2006) 7.

The Only Book With a Blessing

Is your head spinning yet? Over the last two chapters, we've laid out three interpretive keys—understanding Revelation's style, symbols and structure—and maybe you're thinking, "This study of Revelation sounds like a lot of work."

To be honest, it does take some mental effort to read Revelation well. You will have to think, but with these interpretive keys in your hand, it's doable. You may not understand everything, but you'll get the big ideas. You will definitely hear God's message. If you're willing to do the work, here's the promise: you will be blessed.

Revelation is the only book in the New Testament with a specific blessing attached to its reading: "Blessed is the one who reads the words of this prophecy, and blessed are those who hear it and take to heart what is written in it, because the time is near" (Rev 1:3). I don't know all the ways God will use your study to bless you, but as you read, I wouldn't be surprised if you find that your faith is invigorated, your hope is affirmed, your character is refined, your resolve is strengthened, your worship is revived, your witness is ignited, your heart is encouraged, your spiritual eyes are opened and your love for Christ is deepened.

Simply put, Revelation is revolution. This Bible book will transform your life, and nothing will ever be the same again.

Let's start reading the text.

DISSCUSSION QUESTIONS
Chapter 3
You Will Be Blessed

1. Name a time Scripture has encouraged you, challenged you or equipped you.

2. What fears do you have about studying Revelation? What are some good reasons to study it?

3. Have you ever thought of your life as utterly ordinary? How would it change your life if you discovered you were part of an epic story?

4. What possibiities excit you about this study? What kind of "teaching, rebuking, correctin and training in righteousness" might God want to do in your life (2 Tim 3:36)?

CHAPTER FOUR
ENCOUNTER CHRIST POWERFULLY
Revelation 1

"Anyone who has tried to systematize the man Jesus Christ has had, in the end, to admit that the seams keep bursting. He sooner or later discovers that he is in touch, not with a pale Galilean, but with a towering, and furious figure who will not be managed."
— Thomas Howard —

I am a BUICK.

Not the car. BUICK stands for Brought Up In Church Kid, and that's my story. I grew up in a wonderful Christian home, went to church every Sunday and Wednesday, and won the VBS memory verse contest every summer. So I knew what Jesus looked like. After all, as a child, I saw lots of pictures of Jesus. (If you are a BUICK, do you remember flannelgraph?)

Without exception, these pictures showed a gentle Jesus: long, flowing brown hair, white robe, blue sash, lamb around his shoulders, children on his lap, a faint smile upon his lips. This was a meek Jesus, a mild Jesus, a Mr. Rogers Jesus. I could almost picture him in a cardigan sweater, singing "Won't you be my neighbor?" He had kind eyes and went around teaching people to be nice. Yes, I knew what Jesus looked like.

I am also a child of the '80s.

Which means I also knew what a tough guy looked like. When you said the words "action hero," I immediately thought of names like Chuck Norris, Sylvester Stallone, Mr. T, Arnold Schwarzenegger, and Clint Eastwood. These were guys with square jaws, muscled arms, ice water in their veins and eyes as hard as steel. They played cops, boxers, mercenaries, fortune hunters and special-ops soldiers, and they packed enough firepower to take out any enemy. These were guys you didn't mess with, fearsome figures who sparked dread in their adversary's heart, men whose friends and allies respectfully called him "Sir."

When I was a kid, if you had asked me to name the top five most fearsome men I could think of, I would not have mentioned Jesus.

Your God Is Too Small

I'm afraid there are too many Christians who wouldn't list him either.

Don't get me wrong: I'm not saying Jesus should be thought of as some kind of divine Dirty Harry or righteous Rambo. But maybe Jesus is more dangerous than some of us think. J. B. Phillips once wrote a book entitled *Your God Is Too Small*, and my hunch is that many believers today have a mental image of Christ that just isn't big enough. They have put the Second Person of the Trinity in their theological dryers and shrunk him down to become our XL Buddy.

He was a guy with some miraculous powers to be sure, but mostly—to quote William Willimon—they picture Jesus as some "itinerant therapist who, for free, traveled about helping people feel better."[1] Their image of Jesus is closer to Joel Osteen than John Wayne—nice guy, but not much help in a fight. Jesus is a faithful friend, but not a formidable foe.

Too often, the contemporary church suffers from a condition that someone dubbed J.D.D.—Jesus Deficit Disorder.[2] It's not that we don't think about Jesus; it's that we don't think big enough about Jesus. It's like we're seeing him through the wrong end of the telescope—he looks smaller than he really is. A. W. Tozer said, "What comes into our minds when we think about God is the most important thing about us," and my fear is that, for too many of us, our default mental picture is Flannelgraph Jesus.

Churches Gone Astray

Question: What happens when your Jesus is too small?

Answer: Churches like the ones in Revelation 2-3.

When you read through the letters to the seven churches in Asia Minor, you quickly figure out there are two crises afflicting the churches in Asia Minor. The first might be called *the crisis of familiarity*.

Some of these churches are beset with sin. Ephesus has lost its first love (2:4). False teaching has infiltrated the congregation at Pergamum (2:15). Both Pergamum and Thyatira have some who have fallen into idol worship and sexual immorality (2:14, 20). Sitting in the

---

1. William Willimon, "Been There, Preached That" *Leadership* (Fall 1995) 76.
2. Leonard Sweet and Frank Viola, *The Jesus Manifesto* (Nashville: Thomas Nelson, 2010) xv.

pews at Sardis are full-blown hypocrites, people who look spiritually alive but whose faith has no pulse (3:1). Laodicea is lukewarm—complacent and proudly self-sufficient (3:16).

These are some seriously messed up churches. As a young man, John had seen the Church at its start. In Acts, those first believers were a tight-knit community deeply in love with Jesus. They were marked by deep faith, radical obedience, contagious generosity, and bold witness. But now as an old man, John sees churches that have lost their way.

What happened?

They had lost sight of Jesus. They had become too familiar with him to see him for who he really is.

Three Dollars Worth Of God

A. W. Tozer wrote:

> The history of mankind will probably show that no people has ever risen above its religion, and man's spiritual history will positively demonstrate that no religion has ever been greater than its idea of God. Worship is pure or base as the worshiper entertains high or low thoughts of God.[3]

In other words, a diminished vision of Christ leads to a diminished church. A low view of Jesus produces a low life for Jesus. I think that's what happened to the churches of Asia Minor. Oh, they had heard all the stories about Christ, but somehow all they saw was Mr. Rogers Jesus. If your vision of Christ is closer to "action hero"—a steel-fisted, intimidating figure that nobody messes with—you would be too fearful of his judgment to risk such blatant and repeated sin.

But these churches apparently saw Jesus as a much more accommodating deity. They were so familiar with Jesus that he no longer left them awestruck. Jesus was not fearsome or dangerous. They had reduced the King of the Universe to someone who was "nice to have around." In a piece laced with sarcasm, Wilbur Rees describes the heart of such a person.

> I would like to buy $3 worth of God, please. Not enough to explode my soul or disturb my sleep, but just enough to equal a cup of warm milk or a snooze in the sunshine. I don't want enough of God to make me love a black man or pick beets with a migrant. I want ecstasy, not transformation. I want the warmth of the womb, not a new birth. I want a pound of the Eternal in a paper sack. I would like to buy $3 worth of God, please."[4]

---

3. A.W. Tozer, *The Knowledge of the Holy* (New York: HarperCollins, 1978) 1.
4. As quoted in Charles Swindoll, *Improving Your Serve* (Dallas: Word, 1981) 29.

It seems this was the attitude of the churches in Asia Minor. They were apparently not the least bit uncomfortable in Christ's presence. Their Jesus was tame and safe, and when you declaw the Lion of Judah, when you turn him into a warm and fuzzy household pet, who is going to stop you from living however you want? When you no longer see Christ in his terrifying, soul-exploding holiness—you're only one step away from sin.

A Tidal Wave Of Glory

So in Revelation 1, Jesus fixes that.

In this beginning chapter, we find John exiled on the prison island of Patmos. It's the Lord's Day, so John is having his own personal worship service, when suddenly a sound splits the air. A deep, thundering voice—so powerful John can feel it rumble in his chest—commands him, "Write on a scroll what you see and send it to the seven churches: to Ephesus, Smyrna, Pergamum, Thyatira, Sardis, Philadelphia and Laodicea" (Rev 1:11).

When John turns to see the voice, what does John see? He sees what Jesus really looks like, in glorious and dreadful detail:

- Jesus is standing among "seven golden lampstands" representing the seven churches of Asia Minor. He is not off somewhere in the clouds—"the man upstairs" far removed from our lives. "Christ is not an absentee landlord."[5] He is in the midst of his people.
- He looks "like a son of man." John is echoing Daniel 7:13—a stunning vision of the Second Person of the Trinity in all his authority. Jesus is not simply the teacher who hung out with fisherman; he is the one equal to "the Ancient of Days" (Dan 7:13-14).
- He is "dressed in a robe reaching down to his feet and with a golden sash around his chest." This was the clothing of a king. The simple Jewish rabbi has thrown aside the rags of his earthly existence to reveal his true identity—Almighty Sovereign of the Universe.
- "His head and hair were white like wool, as white as snow." Jesus' white hair is not the mark of frailty or aging, but a symbol of his deity and his dignity. He is regal, wise and respect is due him (Dan 7:9; Prov 16:31).

---

5. Metzger, 26.

- This Jesus has eyes "like blazing fire," piercing through our "shams and hypocrisies, looking into our innermost selves."[6]
- His feet "like bronze glowing in a furnace" represent his strength and stability. (Contrast Daniel 2:33, 41.) He will not stumble, trip or falter. He is solid and immovable. Jesus stands firm.
- His voice "was like the sound of rushing waters" — the expression Ezekiel used to describe the voice of God Himself (Ez 43:2).
- "In his right hand he held seven stars." We sing "He's got the whole world in his hands," but here Jesus holds the equivalent of *multiple* worlds — an entire planetary system. He's big.
- "Out of his mouth came a sharp double-edged sword." As the weapon of Rome, the sword represented authority. Here Jesus possesses final authority. The world respects power that comes out of the mouth of a gun, but ultimate power comes out of the mouth of Christ.[7]
- "His face was like the sun shining in all its brilliance." Glory pours forth from Christ, and like one walking from darkness into full sunlight, we are almost blinded by his radiance.

This is not a Jesus in whose presence you can casually stand around, and upon seeing this vision of Christ, John falls at his feet as though dead! Remember: if Jesus had a best friend during his earthly ministry, it was John. John was "the disciple Jesus loved," the one who knew him so well and felt so comfortable with the Savior that he had reclined on Jesus' chest at the Last Supper.

But now, this revelation of Christ in all his splendor washes over John and knocks him face down on the ground. The glory crushes him like a tidal wave and leaves him fighting for his very breath. He is terrified.

Niagara Thunder

This is not the gentle Jesus with children on his lap. This Jesus speaks in Niagara thunder! He blazes with supernova brilliance. This Jesus is so huge that he could play kickball with our planet! He could, with a flick of his finger, send our solar system spinning off into space. This Jesus is the God of Genesis 1, Isaiah 40 and John 1 who created the

---

6. *Ibid.*, 27.
7. Eugene Peterson, *Reversed Thunder* (San Francisco: Harper Collins, 1988) 38.

world—who took a handful of syllables and spoke 10,000 galaxies into existence. With one more word, he could dissolve them all in the heat of a billion nuclear blasts. This Jesus is clothed in glory and splendor, strength and majesty, power and authority. He reigns supreme, and he will tolerate no rivals.

For the churches in Asia Minor, shot through with worldliness, the point is clear: be warned! Jesus is not a kindly grandfather who tussles our hair when we misbehave and says, "Well, boys will be boys." Jesus is not a smiling buddy who winks at our sin and lets us do what we want. He is a "towering and furious figure who will not be managed." He is Lord! He is in the midst of his Church, he knows our sin, and he is big enough to do something about it.

The message to the churches: the next time you're tempted to unholiness in your lifestyle, the next time you're tempted to laziness in your mission, behold the true Christ!!

So what about you? Have you grown too familiar with Jesus? When my wife Katie and I were married in May of 1991, I wanted to take her someplace exotic for our honeymoon.

So I took her to Kansas City.

I was a poor college student—it was the best I could do. While there, we learned that the movie *Mr. and Mrs. Bridge,* starring Paul Newman, had been filmed in Kansas City several months before, and a story was still circulating that caught my attention. Apparently, a woman entered a Haagen-Dazs on the Kansas City Plaza for an ice-cream cone. While she was ordering, another customer entered the store. She placed her order, turned and found herself staring face to face with Paul Newman, who was in town filming the movie. His famous blue eyes made her knees buckle. He said, "Hello." Speechless, she simply nodded at him. She managed to finish paying and quickly walked out of the store with her heart still pounding.

Regaining her composure, she suddenly realized she didn't have her cone; she turned to go back in. At the door she met Paul Newman, who was coming out. He said to her, "Are you looking for your ice cream cone?" Still unable to utter a word, she nodded yes.

"You put it in your purse with your change."

Crash Helmets

We laugh at such a story, and we can identify with that woman. When we are in the presence of someone we deem important, we get a little nervous. Our heart beats faster, our palms sweat, our tongue gets tied, and we might do something a little silly.

Let me ask you: when you walk into the sanctuary on a Sunday morning, does your pulse quicken? Do you catch your breath? Do your palms begin to sweat? Do you get a little nervous?

You should. You are in the presence of the Most Important Person in the Cosmos, none other than the High King of Heaven himself. Perhaps it's time you recover your awe. Annie Dillard writes:

> Why do we people in churches seem like cheerful, brainless tourists on a packaged tour of the Absolute? Does anyone have the foggiest idea what sort of power we so blithely invoke? The churches are children playing on the floor with their chemistry sets, mixing up a batch of TNT to kill a Sunday morning. It is madness to wear ladies' straw hats and velvet hats to church; we should all be wearing crash helmets. Ushers should issue life preservers and signal flares; they should lash us to our pews.[8]

One day Ananias and Sapphira walked into the sanctuary, unmindful of Christ's power. They dared to lie to a Holy God, were struck dead, and "great fear seized the whole church" (Acts 5:11). That is what John's vision of Christ in Revelation 1 is intended to do—to shake us out of our complacency and fill our hearts with worshipful fear.

"Don't Worry—I've Got the Keys"

You may remember that I mentioned two crises afflicting the churches of Asia Minor. If the first was the crisis of familiarity, what's the second? *The crisis of fear.* While some of these churches were blending in to their cultural surroundings, complacent and compromised, a few of the churches were staunchly obedient to Christ . . . and they were taking a beating for it. Family rejection, jobs lost, lives threatened, believers killed. These persecuted churches had "little strength" left (Rev 3:8), and they were afraid (Rev 2:10).

So Jesus' words to John at the end of chapter 1 are words they desperately needed to hear. After John falls on his face in terror at

---

8. Annie Dillard, *Teaching a Stone to Talk* (New York: Harper and Row, 1982) 52.

the glorified Christ, Jesus reaches out tenderly, puts a hand on John's shoulder and says, "Do not be afraid. I am the First and the Last. I am the Living One. I was dead, and behold I am alive for ever and ever! And I hold the keys of death and Hades" (Rev 1:17-18).

How reassuring! This great big Jesus is terrifying, but he is also comforting. To these suffering believers, this vision reminds them that Jesus is more powerful than any problem they encounter, stronger than any foe they face. When they overhear Jesus' words to John, they take heart:

> "Hey John, don't be afraid. It's me! Jesus! The one you loved. You already know me. I'm your old friend. Don't be afraid. The Son of Man, the Ancient of Days, the Alpha and the Omega, the First and the Last, the ruler of the kings of the earth, the one who went to the cross. It's me! It's Jesus!
>
> "By the way, do you remember death and Hades? The ultimate enemies of humankind that have kept them locked in a prison of fear and aloneness from their birth? Here are the keys. Got 'em from my dad. No one who follows me is going to be trapped by death – not one of my friends. I've got the keys. Death? It's no big deal. I've been dead, and it hasn't slowed me down at all."[9]

Maybe that's the word you need to hear today. If you are afraid, here is the good news: it is not a flannelgraph figure looking out for you. It is the almighty Christ. In the movies, if the "action hero" is on your team, you have nothing to fear. In real life, the one you want at your side is Jesus.

By the way, as we close, remember how Revelation 1 begins. The very first words of the chapter are: "The revelation of Jesus Christ" (Rev 1:1). That's the purpose of this book – to reveal Jesus.

Do you see him?

---

9. John Ortberg, *Everybody's Normal Till You Get to Know Them* (Grand Rapids: Zondervan, 2003) 232.

Disscussion Questions
Chapter 4
Encounter Christ Powerfully

1. What has been your mental pictures of Jesus?
   How does the Revelation 1 description of Jesus compare to what you hear in our culture? What you hear in church?

2. What do you think happens when our concept of Christ is too small?

3. Would you say you're more susceptible to the crisis of familiarity or the crisis of fear? What happens when we succumb to either one?

4. Which of Christ's attributes here seize your attention? Which unsettle you? Which confort you?

CHAPTER FIVE
LOVE THE CHURCH HONESTLY
Revelation 2-3

*"Call it a clan, call it a tribe, call it a network, call it a family.
Whatever you call it, whoever you are, you need one."*
— Jane Howard —

Several years ago, two of my nephews accompanied their mom on a visit to a friend's house. Ben was 8, Brian was 6. Their mother's friend was a very neat lady — a place for everything and everything in its place. She had defeated clutter and driven it from her home. Though childless, she did have a few toys and handed Ben and Brian a bucket of Legos®: "Here boys, you can play with these."

What's the first thing they did with that bucket? Like all red-blooded American boys, they dumped it out. Their mother's uptight friend immediately went into full obsessive-compulsive mode. She dropped to her knees and started scooping the Lego® pieces back into the bucket with these words: "No, no, no, boys. What I meant was, you can play with these . . . one at a time."

What?

You might be able to play with dolls or Hot Wheels® cars one at a time, but *you can't play with Legos® one at time!* A Lego® piece's whole purpose is to be combined with other pieces. A Lego® piece is created to be part of a group, something bigger than itself. A solitary Lego® can never fulfill its destiny. Legos® were made to be connected.

Lego® Theology

You don't have to read far into your Bible to discover: human beings were made to be combined with other human beings. In Genesis 1, God makes the world and declares, "It is good." But after creating a man, God says, "It is not good." Why? Because the man is alone. There's only one of him, and humans aren't meant to do life one at a time. So God decides to split the Adam. (I know, bad joke.) He makes Eve from Adam's rib to be his life-partner, and only then can God say, "It is very good." We were created for community.

Call it Lego® theology: human beings were made to be connected. We are hard-wired for relationship. A solitary human being can never fulfill his destiny. You simply cannot flourish alone. A landmark Harvard study of 7,000 people found that the most isolated people were *three times more likely to die* than those with strong relationships. Reporting on the study, John Ortberg writes that "people who had bad health habits (such as smoking, poor eating habits, or alcohol use) but strong social ties lived *significantly longer* than people who had great health habits but were isolated. In other words, it is better to eat Twinkies with good friends than to eat broccoli alone."[1]

What is true physically is also true spiritually: if we want to maintain a healthy, lifelong walk with Christ, we need community. To stay faithful we must stay connected.

That's why God invented the church.

A Life Lived Together

Unfortunately, too many in our culture want nothing to do with "organized religion." (Although if they visited very many churches, they'd find we're not very organized!) They may say they're committed to Jesus, but they want nothing to do with the church. The title of Philip Yancey's book, *Church: Why Bother?*, describes their attitude. Disillusioned with imperfect congregations, they take a "just-me-and-Jesus" approach: "I'll worship as I hike through the woods and listen to my music. Forget church."

But the very placement of Revelation 2 and 3 will not allow us to do that. Eugene Peterson explains:

> We would prefer to go directly from the awesome vision of Christ (Rev. 1) to the glorious ecstasies of heaven (Rev. 4, 5) ... But we can't do it. The church has to be negotiated first. The only way from Christ to heaven ... is through the church.[2]

Revelation 2 and 3 remind us that, while faith is certainly personal, it is never individual. The vision of Revelation was given *to* John, but it was *for* the church. The message of this book is not for an isolated believer, but for seven congregations! Even a cursory reading of Revelation 2 and 3 teaches us: *Jesus is committed to the church.*

---

1. Ortberg, *Everybody's Normal*, 33.
2. Peterson, *Thunder*, 45.

Jesus didn't begin the Lord's Prayer, "*My* Father who art in heaven." He taught us to pray "*Our* Father" because the Christian life is meant to be a life lived together. Jesus did not simply come to save people; He came to save *a* people — a community of believers. So if you belong to Jesus, you also belong to everyone else who belongs to Jesus. Imperfect as it is, the church is part of the package.

Jesus wants you to stay connected.

Think Global, Act Local

In Revelation 2 and 3, it's important to notice that Jesus does not address these letters to the capital "C" Church in general. He addresses them to specific, local congregations, each one in a different city. Ephesus bustled with commerce. Smyrna's public architecture was renowned for its beauty. Pergamum was known for its learning, with a library that rivaled Alexandria's famous one. Thyatira was filled with craftsmen and artisans. Though still wealthy, Sardis was fading in importance. Philadelphia's economy was agricultural, surrounded by vineyards, but beset by earthquakes. Laodicea served as a regional medical center.

These seven churches are called lampstands (Rev 1:20), each called to light their unique little corner of the globe. Each city is a particular kind of mission field, and each church is made of people who just happen to live in that particular city's geographical region, eat the local food, work in the local economy, know the local customs, and speak the local language. In other words, they are the perfect missionaries to reach their community.

God's global mission is always lived out locally. God doesn't command the church to franchise — with one-size-fits-all, look-exactly-alike operations in every place — because you cultivate the gospel seed differently from one place to another. My friend Dudley preaches in Los Angeles, wears Hawaiian shirts, surfs, and does beach baptisms, while my friend David preaches in small-town Kansas, wears overalls, rebuilds tractors and does hog roasts. Both churches, though different in approach, are effective and growing because they're well suited to reach their particular community. God's idea to plant *local* churches is genius.

True Community Begins With Disillusionment

But let's be honest: local little "c" churches never live up to God's grand and glorious idea called the capital "C" Church. When we read books like Acts and Ephesians, we catch God's vision for this vibrant community called Church. It's meant to be a band of believers ablaze with love for Christ, a hospital welcoming wounded sinners, a little Bible college digging deeply into Scripture together, an army of prayer warriors storming the gates of heaven, a missionary outpost taking the gospel to all those around them. Who wouldn't want to be a part of that? Sign me up!

Then we walk into our local congregation, and find ourselves disappointed:

> We expect a disciplined army of committed men and women who courageously lay siege to the worldly powers; instead we find some people who are more concerned with getting rid of the crabgrass in their lawns. We expect a community of saints who are mature in the virtues of love and mercy, and find ourselves working on a church supper where there is more gossip than there are casseroles.[3]

When we discover that our local congregation falls short of expectations, we sometimes wash our hands of them and move on, looking for the ideal church. We are like the girl who broke up with her boyfriend with these words: "I will always cherish the initial misconception I had about you." Ouch!

But real love doesn't happen in fantasy; it happens in reality. You can't love someone for who you wish they were; you must love them as they actually are, flaws and all. Dietrich Bonhoeffer said that true Christian community *begins* with disillusionment. You aren't really loving your Christian brothers until they've disappointed you and you choose to stick by them anyway. Only then does true relationship start.

That's exactly what Jesus does for the churches in Revelation 2-3. He models for us an unconditional love for imperfect churches. He cares about these individual congregations--each particular group of people with all their unique tastes and habits, customs and culture, quirks and faults, annoyances and charmes.

Jesus wants you to learn to love a local church too.

And what will happen when you do? Jesus will give you the same three gifts he gave to the Asian churches in these letters: *affirmation, correction* and *promise.*

---

3. *Ibid.*, 55.

In the Church We Are Given Affirmation

Some time ago, my wife Katie and I were rummaging through an attic box of old college keepsakes. I reached for a large manila envelope, wondering what was inside. Old love letters! I pulled out a thick stack of envelopes Katie had sent me one summer when we were dating.

We were apart all summer, and I remember waiting eagerly for those twice-a-week letters in the mail. I would tear open the envelope and devour every sentence—reading and rereading every word, imagining the voice of my beloved speaking them to me. The letter read "Dear Matt," but behind the words I could hear her heart's true message—"my handsome hunk of a guy." I loved getting those letters!

(By the way, Katie reached into the box and pulled out a manila envelope . . . with both of the letters I wrote her that summer. Yes, I am a slob.)

Those letters were a tonic for my soul. Being apart all summer, it would have been easy for me to believe Katie wasn't thinking of me. "Out of sight, out of mind." But in her letters, she would mention something she appreciated about me or something she knew I was doing that particular week. Psychiatrist M. Scott Peck says, "The principal form that the work of love takes is attention," and those letters were Katie's way of paying attention to me.

The persecuted churches of Asia Minor might have believed that Jesus had forgotten about them, but these letters are a tangible reminder: Jesus was paying attention to them. In these letters, he says, "I know your situation," and Christ affirms some quality he sees: untiring labor (Ephesus), brave suffering (Smyrna), faithful witness (Pergamum), growing devotion (Thyatira), and steadfast endurance (Philadelphia).

In a world that applauds those with money, political power, athletic prowess, and sex appeal, Jesus here commends an entirely different set of values. He affirms the quiet, unnoticed, faithful lives of his people and celebrates these believers as heaven's heroes.

This is a gift we need.

The media mocks us, politicians discriminate against us, skeptics attack us, and hostile forces seek to destroy us. But when we come together as the church, we are reminded that Jesus cares deeply about us, and no matter what our culture thinks, he sees us as significant.

In the church, we are given the affirming love of Christ. Stay connected.

In the Church We Are Given Correction

While some of these congregations are threatened by physical persecution, others are in greater danger of cultural seduction. Some have begun to compromise their faith. So to each church in Asia Minor (except Smyrna and Philadelphia), Jesus also gives a word of correction.

"I have this against you," Christ says—but do not mistake His directness for hostility. In *The Last Lecture*, Randy Pausch writes, "When you're screwing up and nobody says anything to you anymore, that means they've given up on you." Jesus' words are tough love, to be sure, but they are love nonetheless. He has not given up on them. Jesus specifically calls out five sinful patterns he sees developing. Do any of these sound familiar?

- *Lost Passion.* The Ephesian church had lost their first love. Though still faithful, their desire for Christ had cooled, like a marriage dulled by years of routine. Has your hunger for the Word waned? Your passion for prayer diminished? Is your service more duty than joy?
- *False Teaching.* In Pergamum and Thyatira, believers faced enormous pressure to join the cultural ritual of idol worship. (If not, they could lose their jobs.) So when the false teachers lowered God's standards on idolatry, their words were welcome. Still today, feel-good, low-demand faith sells lots of books, attracts lots of TV viewers and builds huge "churches."
- *Sexual Immorality.* In Pergamum and Thyatira, sexual immorality had crept into the church. This remains one of Satan's most effective strategies. Adultery, premarital sex, pornography—almost every week I hear of another brother or sister who's fallen.
- *Spiritual Hypocrisy.* The church at Sardis has a reputation for being spiritually alive, but is dead inside. Their faith is a façade. These folks can swear at their kids Saturday night and sing hymns Sunday morning, carefully practicing image management to look spiritual.
- *Materialism.* Laodicea's faith is lukewarm because they are serving two masters: God and money. Jesus has no word of affirmation for this materialistic church—which is scary, because this is the congregation the American church most resembles. We too are wealthy, and it's hard to trust God for our daily bread when our pantry's already full.

We Cannot Become Ourselves By Ourselves

I'm confident these churches did not begin this way. At one time, I imagine these congregations were closer to the movement in Acts 2 than the mess in Revelation 2. I am sure they didn't intend to become ineffective and disobedient.

No one wakes up one morning and says, "Today I'd like to fall pray to false teaching."

No one says their wedding vows thinking, "I hope I become an adulterer someday."

No one enters the waters of baptism intending to be a half-hearted, passionless Christian.

No one makes it their goal to lapse into shallow and lukewarm materialism.

No one as a child plans to be a two-faced hypocrite when they grow up.

No one plans these things, and yet they happen every day. Why? At least one reason: no one else spoke up. We all have blind spots—areas where we are not living up to God's intention for our lives and of which we are unaware. If we are to avoid lifewreck, we need someone else to speak up, to lovingly confront us, to call us to be the person God made us to be. As a wise man once said, "We cannot become ourselves by ourselves."

That is the gift we receive as part of the church. When we gather as God's people, Christ speaks to us through His preached Word, rebuking and correcting our sin. In the church, a Christian brother or sister can put an arm around our shoulder and tenderly say, "I'm concerned about where I see you heading." Author Gordon MacDonald tells of such a time when he was in Japan with a close friend:

> He was a number of years older than I was. As we walked down the street in Yokohama, Japan, the name of a common friend came up, and I said something unkind about that person. It was sarcastic. It was cynical. It was a put-down. My older friend stopped, turned, and faced me. With deep, slow words he said, "Gordon, a man who says he loves God would not say a thing like that about a friend."
>
> He could have put a knife into my ribs, and the pain would not have been any less. But you know something? There have been ten thousand times in the last twenty years that I have been saved from making a jerk of myself. When I've been tempted to say something unkind about a brother or sister, I hear my friend's voice say, "Gordon, a man who says he loves God would not speak in such a way about a friend."[4]

---

4. Gordon MacDonald, "Feeling as God Feels," *Preaching Today* 196

Hard as it may be to receive, such a word of correction can save us. Like a scalpel, it can cut out the cancer that threatens our soul. If we are to stay faithful over the long haul, we need this gift.

In the church, we are given the loving correction of Christ. Stay connected.

In the Church We Are Given a Promise

In each letter, Christ closes by describing a heavenly reward for the "one who overcomes." These motivating promises each picture a part of our new life in heaven. We will eat from the tree of life in paradise, wear the crown of life, remain untouched by the second death, receive a new name, be given the morning star, wear white robes, hear our name spoken by Jesus before the Father, gain a permanent place in the temple of God, and sit on Christ's throne with him. Wow!

Do you think this was an encouragement to these struggling churches? Overwhelmed and under siege, they desperately needed a word of promise. As humans, we can survive three weeks without food, three days without water, three minutes without air, but we cannot survive three seconds without hope. Hope is the oxygen of the soul. The old Baptist preacher Vance Havner used to say, "The hope of dying is the only thing that keeps me alive!" Christ's promises of heaven breathed new life into these suffering saints.

We too need these promises to persevere. In a culture focused on the here and now, we need to be reminded that the life worth living is the one set on "things above" (Col 3:2). In the church, we are given these reminders.

During the Lord's Supper, we gather at a table that looks forward to another Table—the wedding banquet of the Lamb. We sing songs that promise "some glad morning when this life is o'er, I'll fly away." We read Scriptures that tell of "an inheritance that can never perish, spoil or fade—kept in heaven for you" (1 Pet 1:4). The simple act of gathering on Sunday—Jesus' resurrection day—reminds us of our approaching resurrection day, and as we remember, we gain strength to follow Christ for another week.

In the church, we are given the motivating promises of Christ that help us stay faithful.

Stay connected.

DISSCUSSION QUESTIONS
Chapter 5
Love The Church Honestly

1. How woud you describe your experience in a local church? Why do you think some people who love Jesus avoid church? What are some perils of the solitary Christian life?

2. Which of the struggles in the Asia Minor churches are true of the American church? Which strengths? Which are true of your local church?

3. Have you ever received a word of correction? How did it go? Now tell about a word of affirmation you received and what it meant to you.

4. What is your local church doing to uniquely reach your local community?

CHAPTER SIX

WORSHIP GOD WHOLEHEARTEDLY

Revelation 4-5

*"Your most profound experiences of worship
will likely be on your darkest days."*
—Rick Warren—

My wife and I have six kids. Can I tell you what Sunday mornings are like at my house? I'd like to tell you they are a time of joy and focused preparation. I'd like to tell you that I wake up at 5:30 a.m. with a smile on my face, roll over to kiss my wife (with minty fresh breath) and say, "Good morning, dear. It is the Lord's Day. Let us arise and worship!" I'd like to say that I hop out of bed, do 100 pushups and then (barely winded), I walk into the bathroom to comb my hair. But lo, it has not moved during the night.

I'd like to tell you that I put on my three-piece suit and go to the kitchen where my wife and I squeeze oranges to make homemade orange juice as we recite memory verses to one another. I'd like to tell you that my six children—ages 19, 17, 14, 11, 9 and 5—all walk into the kitchen, having dressed themselves, and say with smiles upon their faces, "Good morning, mother. Good morning, father. It is the Lord's Day. Let us arise and worship!" I'd like to tell you that we then get into the van and drive the 15 minutes to church, singing together as a family "How Great Thou Art."

But it would be a big, fat lie.

Not Ready For Worship

Sunday mornings at my house are crazy! Rush and hustle, and no matter how early we get up, it seems we're always running late. I hate running late! Since I'm being honest, I'll tell you: I can start to lose my cool with my kids. I'm hurriedly slapping the cold cereal into their breakfast bowls, milk spilling on the table, and I find myself barking orders at them with ever increasing volume:

"You, hurry up and eat!"

"You, go get your clothes on!"

"You, stop crying!"

"You, stop hitting your sister!"

"Yes, you have to wear clothes to church!"

"You, go get your Bible!"

"You, go comb your hair!"

"Come on, kids, CHOP, CHOP! Let's GO! We're LATE! I need you to get out in the van RIGHT NOW! Hurry UP! NOW! WE'VE GOT TO GO TO CHURCH AND LEARN ABOUT THE LOVE OF GOD!!"

After the mad scramble for the van, I roar out of the driveway, red-faced, smoke pouring out of my ears, shaking my head, muttering under my breath, driving 175 mph. We screech into the parking lot, I slam open the van door and herd my children along like an impatient prison guard with a chain gang.

Of course, there's always the greeter at the door, so I momentarily paste on a smile as I shake his hand, "Good morning, brother. It is the Lord's Day. Let us arise and worship!" But then I walk into the sanctuary with a pounding pulse, clouded mind and irritated soul, and I am certainly not focused on God.

I am not ready to worship.

Am I the only one with Sunday mornings like this? Maybe you've been there. It's easy to be distracted during worship — by family issues or work problems or financial worries or even the misspelled PowerPoint slide.

Let's be clear: the churches in Asia Minor faced more than distraction. They faced harassment, even possible execution. Gathering to worship was not simply inconvenient. It was potentially dangerous. They weren't walking into the sanctuary with elevated blood pressure because it was hard getting their kids ready that morning. They walked in wondering how to protect their children from real harm.

It wouldn't be surprising if they lost their enthusiasm for worship.

Worship First, Ask Questions Later

But when we feel like worshipping the least is when we need to worship the most.

John knew that. The white-haired old apostle found himself exiled on a prison island, far from family and friends, left alone to die. But rather than growing bitter or giving in to self-pity, John entered whatever makeshift sanctuary he could find on Patmos on the Lord's Day, and he was "in the Spirit" (Rev 1:10). He chose to worship.

In Revelation 4-5, John's readers are about to enter the sanctuary with him. The door is standing open waiting (Rev 4:1), but before his readers push through, surely a question begs to be answered.

Why now?

The question of suffering must have dominated their thoughts. Why was a good God letting bad things happen to them? If they were obeying Jesus, why were they getting put in prisons and on crosses? This was surely the conversation John's readers wanted to have first — an explanation for the evil they've encountered, some answers to the problem of their pain. Their questions are important, and in chapter 6, Revelation will turn to the problem of evil. But before that, in Revelation 4 and 5, they will first be ushered into worship.

Why is it so important to worship first? Why does John seem to be telling us that the worst moments of our life are the best moments to worship?

These chapters reveal three reasons: worship *centers* us, *unites* us, and *heartens* us.

Worship Centers Us

April 15, 1865. The day after President Lincoln's assassination, a crowd gathered on the streets in New York City. The news had inflamed emotions, and the mood was angry toward those in the city who had been critical of the President. Cries for vengeance began to sound. As the throng threatened to become a mob, suddenly a man stepped forward, and despite his ramrod posture, few knew this former Union Army general. But his strong, clear voice rang out, and his commanding presence galvanized attention: "Fellow citizens! Clouds and darkness are around about Him. His pavilion is dark waters and thick clouds of the skies. Justice and judgment are the establishment of his throne. Mercy and truth shall go before His face. Fellow citizens! God reigns, and the government at Washington still lives!"

These words immediately calmed the crowd, averting violence. The speaker was Major General James A. Garfield, congressman from Ohio. Garfield, a Christian Church preacher, went on to become the only clergyman to ever serve as President of the United States.

In the midst of insecurities and tumult, Garfield knew what the people needed to hear: God is still on His throne.

The apostle John knew this too.

When life seems filled with uncertainties, we need a center, an anchor, a firm and fixed point from which we can navigate. For the sailor, it's the North Star. For the musician, it's middle C.

For the Christian, it's the throne.

"Throne" is the key word in chapter 4, used 14 times. It might be the key word to the entire book, appearing 46 times. The bedrock of Christian theology is the sovereignty of God. It is the conviction that our God is in control of the universe. Our God reigns, and in worship, God's supremacy is once again impressed upon our minds.

It happens in Revelation 4 and 5

Left Speechless . . .

When you walk through the open door in Revelation 4, you enter the throne room of heaven. You suck in your breath, shield your eyes from the dazzling light and drop to your knees in fear and wonder. Incense fills your nostrils. An angelic warhost so vast you have to count it by the ten thousands shakes the very foundations of the sky with their praise. The countless thundering voices rumble in your chest. The noise is so loud you can't hear yourself think.

As you trace their attention, you find that every being in heaven is focused on the throne. At the center of that throne is a majestic God — so holy that he cannot be named, so glorious that the only way John can paint him is by dipping his brush in thunder, lightning, rainbows and jewels.

If we wanted, we could try to take apart the imagery of this scene. We could say that the flashing crystal clarity of jasper and the blood-red smoldering fire of carnelian hint at God's blazing, pure holiness. We could say that the rainbow encircling the throne — harking back to God's Genesis promise to withhold flood-judgment — portrays His faithful mercies. We could say the crashing thunder, splitting lightning, and conquered sea (as smooth as glass) all signify God's majestic power.

But mostly we are meant to say nothing at all. John's finite words cannot hope to capture infinite realities — like attempting to reproduce the Mona Lisa with crayons—but he is pushing language to the breaking point, intending to leave us without language.

We are meant to be left speechless.

We are also meant to be left fearless.

The vision of God on the throne is meant to recalibrate our imagination, "swiveling the universe on the hinges of a single image."[1] John's readers thought the world was controlled by Emperor Domitian. Maybe you know the feeling: when you are assailed by doubts and dangers, fear can loom large in your mind, blotting out the blue sky of heaven. Your worries invade you like a hostile army, innumerable and unconquerable.

But in worship, we see the throne, and these earthly fears assume their proper size. In light of God's power, they are frail and finite. Our entire outlook on the world changes. This worship scene declares, "Be encouraged, small, persecuted church. Be warned, haughty Roman empire. Tremble with fear, Satan and your host of darkness. God is on the throne and he is in the center of all things!"[2]

Worship centers us on our all-powerful God.

Worship Unites Us

Worship does more than center us on God's sovereignty. It also unites us with God's Creation.

Several years ago, Christian musician Chris Rice wrote a tune called "The Cartoon Song." This satirical little song wondered tongue-in-cheek what it would be like "if cartoons got saved" and started singing "hallelujah" praise to God. Imagine an upbeat, playful melody and the cartoon voice imitations as he sings:

Fred and Wilma Flintstone sing, "Yabba-dabba-lujah!"
Scooby-doo and Shaggy: "Scooby-dooby-lujah!"
And the Jetsons' dog named Astro: "Ru-ro-rujah!"
Teenage Mutant Ninja Turtles: "Cowabunga-lujah, Dude!"

Then there's, "Kermit the Frog here, singing, Hi-ho-a-lujah."
And that little bald guy, Elmer Fudd: "How-wa-wujah."
Oh and that big old moose and his friend Rocky, "Bullwinkle-lujah"
And our favorite bear named Yogi, "Hey, Boo-Boo-lujah"

---

1. Thomas Long, *Preaching and the Literary Forms of the Bible* (Philadelphia: Fortress, 1989) 47.
2. Scotty Smith and Michael Card, *Unveiled Hope* (Nashville: Thomas Nelson, 1997) 69.

When it came on the radio, my kids and I laughed and sang along. The song was a fun way to make a serious point: "There's a lot of praisin' to do, and cartoons weren't made for that. It's our job. So let's sing hallelujah."

But maybe . . . Chris Rice was on to something. Maybe we shouldn't laugh at the idea of a frog, two dogs, four turtles, a moose and a bear singing praise to God. Maybe more than simply humans were made to bring God praise.

John would agree. Once you tear your eyes from God's throne in Revelation 4 and look around, the images John describes could almost look like cartoon figures singing hallelujah. The throne stands at the center of the heavenly scene, and John paints a picture of beings in concentric circles moving out from the throne.

In the first circle are four living creatures, representing all categories of creation; the noblest (lion), strongest (ox), wisest (human) and swiftest (eagle) all continually give glory to God (Rev 4:6-8). They are at their most alive as they worship—constantly alert (covered with eyes) and immensely powerful (six wings)—and these creatures picture the Biblical truth of Psalm 96:13, "Let all creation rejoice before the Lord." Doves and iguanas, cacti and lilies, tigers and silk worms, dwarf stars and oak trees and dolphins and thoroughbreds all pulse with praise to their Maker.

In Genesis 3, when sin entered the world, man's relationship with nature was fractured; plants and animals and natural forces would now resist him. But in worship, we are once again united with the world around us. All Creation sings hallelujah, and when we sing with it, we momentarily look backward to Eden and forward to Paradise when we will be at peace with the created order.

"A Chief Communifying Force"

After the four creatures, the next concentric circle around the throne includes the twenty-four elders (Rev 4:4). Who do they represent? Most likely, they symbolize the Old Testament people of God (twelve tribes of Israel) and the New Testament people of God (twelve apostles). Dressed in white robes and gold crowns, they are seated on thrones, but when the four creatures start their praise song, the twenty-four elders fall to their knees and join in the worship.

Notice that, in worship, all God's people are joined together as one. I know that Bible guys all seem the same to us—they all wear robes and speak a foreign language. But there is actually a vast difference between a middle-eastern desert nomad like Abraham and an urban intellectual Roman citizen like the apostle Paul. Yet here, despite their differences, old covenant and new covenant believers gather to sing in unity.

Worship is a connecting force. It's amazing the things that can divide Christians—Bible translations, political preferences and carpet color for the new building. (Someone facetiously rewrote Matthew 18:20 to read, "Where two or three are gathered in my name ... there's going to be an argument!") However, worship has the power to bind us together as we lift our voices in common song. Congregational singing is, someone said, a "chief communifying force" as people literally "get in tune" with one another.

Worship unites us. In fact, look at the next concentric circle in the heavenly worship scene: angels—numbering in the millions—all singing with heart-piercing beauty (Rev 5:11-12). Then in the last and greatest concentric circle stands "every creature in heaven and on earth and under the earth and on the sea, and all that is in them, singing" (Rev 5:13). Wow!!

In worship we are united with God's creation, God's people, God's angelic servants—united with all the world in giving praise to God. When these small struggling churches gather on Sunday morning to worship, they are joining an orchestra as large as the universe itself. When they struggle with the question of evil, it may seem like the whole world is against them. But when they worship, they are reminded that, in the truest sense, the whole world is with them!

Worship Heartens Us

Worship centers us on God's sovereignty, unites us with God's Creation, and as we'll see, worship also heartens us with God's sacrificial love in Christ.

John notices a sealed scroll in God's hand—seemingly representing God's decreed plan for history. But because no one is found worthy to open the scroll, John's heart is broken. Who will carry out God's plan? Is there anyone worthy? Will God's purposes go unfulfilled? Will his people be left unheeded and unloved? John "wept and wept" (Rev 5:4).

But then an elder seeks to cheer the despairing apostle, "Do not weep! See, the Lion of the tribe of Judah, the Root of David, has triumphed. He is able to open the scroll and its seven seals" (Rev 5:5).

John turns, expecting to see the great and powerful King of the Beasts, but instead he sees the most vulnerable creature of all—a sacrificial Lamb. But this Lamb, though it had been slain, is now standing in the center of the throne gloriously alive—his seven horns signifying perfect power, seven eyes signifying perfect knowledge. Clearly this Lamb is Jesus! Why is the Lion pictured as a Lamb? Because Christ exhibited his strength through weakness. On the cross, he conquered through sacrifice.

Do you think the seven churches find their hearts soaring at God's love demonstrated in Christ on Calvary? Do you think they take note that triumph comes through sacrifice—which means their own sacrifices are achieving victory for them? And do you think they are heartened by the fact that Christ has been where they've been, understands their weakness and knows what it's like to face pain, hostility and death?

In worship, we are reminded of God's love for us in Christ, and we are encouraged.

"Man Of Sorrows"

Joni Eareckson Tada became a quadriplegic after a diving accident at age 17. She tells about Jackie, her best friend in high school and her co-captain on the field hockey team. After a tough loss on the field their senior year, Joni remembers she and Jackie sitting in the back of the team bus, drying their tears and singing together, "Man of Sorrows, what a name, for the Son of God who came." They were glad they had a Savior who understood their heavy hearts.

Three months later, shortly after her high school graduation, Joni dove into shallow water and broke her neck. As she faced lifelong paralysis, suddenly God didn't seem so good any more. She wondered if he truly cared. One night as she lay in the hospital bed, she felt all alone, and she cried out in prayer, "Lord, I can't do this!"

But that was the night her friend Jackie sneaked in to see Joni after hours. She hid behind the couch in the visitors' lounge until the hallway lights went out. As Joni lay wide awake, wrestling with her fears, she suddenly saw Jackie crawling across the linoleum floor into her room. Joni hissed, "Jackie, if they catch you, they are going to kick you out of here!" Jackie said, "Shhhh" and then climbed up into the hospital bed with Joni. She took Joni's hand, and knowing that Joni could feel nothing, Jackie raised it up so her friend could see they were holding hands.

Then Jackie began to softly sing, "Man of Sorrows, what a name, for the Son of God who came, ruined sinners to reclaim. Hallelujah, what a Savior!" In that sacred moment, said Joni, that song "met my need like nothing else. And it underscored how good, how very good God is." In worship, her heart suddenly knew that the God who sent His Son as a sacrificial Lamb understood her pain. He cared.

When you face the problem of pain, the deep mystery of suffering in your life, what do you need the most? You need to be centered on God's sovereignty, united with God's people and heartened by God's love. You need to worship.

When you feel like worshipping the least is when you need to worship the most.

I'll try to remember that next Sunday morning.

DISSCUSSION QUESTIONS
Chapter 6
Worship God Wholeheartedly

1. Have you ever been distracted in worship? How?
   Tell about a favorite or memorable worship experience.

2. Mke a list of God's qualities -- as many as you can think of.
   Which amazes you most?

3. How does worship help us in the trials of life? What fears or
   tummults are in your life now? How would a vision of God on
   his throne affect you?

4. What did you learn about the importance and nature of worship
   from reflectin on Revelation 4-5? How might that change your
   worship in the future?

CHAPTER SEVEN

ENDURE SUFFERING PATIENTLY

Revelation 6-7

*"God had one son on earth without sin,
but never one without suffering."*
—St. Augustine—

In his book *In the Eye of the Storm*, Max Lucado tells the story of Chippy the parakeet. Chippy was the joy of his owner's life, a widow we'll call Mrs. Smith, filling her days with song. One day, while Mrs. Smith was vacuuming, she noticed Chippy's cage was dirty. So she opened the little door and, using her attachment, began to vacuum out the cage bottom as Chippy safely sat on his perch.

Just then the phone rang. As she turned to answer the phone, Mrs. Smith moved the attachment in the cage a little too high and—whoosh! To her horror, she sucked Chippy into the vacuum cleaner! She immediately dropped the phone, turned the vacuum off, tore open the bag, and began to dig for her precious pet. To her amazement, Mrs. Smith found him still alive, stunned, but covered with dust and debris.

Her poor birdie was dirty.

So she grabbed him, raced to the bathroom, turned on the faucet and shoved Chippy under the torrent of cold water. The dirt cascaded off into the sink, but then Mrs. Smith noticed her parakeet was shivering from the water's shock.

Her poor Chippy was drippy.

So she did the only thing that came to mind. Mrs. Smith grabbed her blow dryer and blasted him with hot air to dry him out as quickly as possible. Of course, the volcanic air left Chippy scorched.

Her poor parakeet had felt the heat.

A few days later, a reporter somehow heard of Chippy's ordeal and called Mrs. Smith to get the details of the story. At the end of the call, the reporter asked, "And how is Chippy doing now?"

"Well, physically he seems fine," said Mrs. Smith. "But these days he just kinda sits there. Chippy doesn't sing much anymore." Sometimes life has a way of stealing your song.

From Singing To Suffering

When we walk out of Revelation 4-5, we are singing! We've just been to the most amazing worship service of our lives. But we are barely four verses into Revelation 6 when the song is torn from our lips.

In Revelation 6 and 7, the seals on history's scroll unleash profound calamities—the various types of suffering the world experiences. The Bible points to several different causes of suffering:

- Our own sinful choices (Gal 6:7-8)
- Others' sinful choices (Gen 4:8)
- A fallen world (Rom 8:18-21)
- Satan (Job 2:7, 2 Cor 12:7)
- God himself (Heb 12:4-11; Num 14:26-35)

When we see suffering, there is a danger in confidently assigning each tragedy a cause. Four months ago, my wife was diagnosed with cancer. Did God cause my wife's cancer, or did Satan? Or just a fallen world? I don't know. What we *can* say is this: in his sovereignty, God will use suffering—no matter its direct cause—for his purpose.

The Echo Of Hoofbeats

In the seven seals of Revelation 6-7, the suffering is all under God's control. No matter the specific cause, God is using the chaos to accomplish his desires in history.

In case you're wondering, the catastrophes described here are most likely not a particular future sequence of events. "This is not a description of what *will* take place. Nor is this what *did* take place. This is a description of what *always* takes place."[1] In every age we see these kinds of travails, all of which lead up to the end of time. What kind of suffering do we see?

- *Military invasion.* The first seal looses a bow-carrying horseman "bent on conquest" (Rev 1:2). The feared Parthian warriors to Rome's east were the only mounted archers of the age, so they

---

1. Mark Moore, *How to Dodge a Dragon* (Joplin: College Press, 1998) 40.

immediately came to the original reader's mind. But the first horseman of the apocalypse represents all military invaders, whether Genghis Khan or Nazi Germany, and the violent societal upheaval they inflict.

- *Conflict and bloodshed.* The second seal looses a fiery red horse whose rider carries a large sword, disrupts peace wherever he goes, and causes men to slay each other. "History is a long sequence of battles. The battle rages in family circles; it is contested between nations. War is the human condition."[2] Somewhere every day, someone is killing someone else—in the gang neighborhoods of Chicago or on the battlefields of Afghanistan.
- *Famine.* A quart of wheat is starvation rations for a family, and a denarius is a day's wage—one loaf of bread for $150. Sometimes famine is war's consequence, but sometimes famine is simply the result of a planet with an operating system infected with the virus of sin. Drought strikes, locusts devour, crops fail. Either way, in ancient Palestine or in modern Niger, children starve.
- *Death.* The fourth horseman is Death himself. The echo of his hoofbeats sound in every era, every community, every life. His means are many—sword, famine, disease, wild animals—but the end is always the same: caskets, funerals, graveyards, weeping families left behind. Death is not our friend; he is always an enemy.
- *Christian persecution.* When the fifth seal is opened, we see Christian martyrs who have died for the faith. Every age has seen Christians targeted—by wild beasts unleashed in the Roman Coliseum and by jihad unleashed in an Iranian church.
- *Natural disaster.* Ever since Genesis 3, our planet has been defective: earthquakes, meteors, hurricanes, tsunami, volcanic eruptions, and tornadoes. When nature malfunctions, people are thrown into chaos, and the sixth seal describes such disasters in terrifying apocalyptic language.[3]

The point in all of this is not to identify the exact references described in these seals with pinpoint precision. Rather, the point is simply to be warned: before Jesus comes back, things are going to get bad, and then

---

2. Peterson, Thunder, p. 74.
3. Some scholars believe these catastrophic events are metaphors describing the fall of powerful nations. Similar language is used elsewhere to describe the fall of Babylon (Is 13), Tyre (Is 24), Egypt (Ez 32) and even Jerusalem (Matt 24).

they are going to get worse. While God allows these judgments to fall on unrepentant sinners in the hopes of awakening them, the saints are sometimes unfortunately caught in the crossfire.

Doesn'tmakeyoufeellikesingingmuch,doesit?Howwillweendure?

The fifth and sixth seals reveal two very important questions in the midst of hard times—poignant questions asked out of anguished hearts. In Revelation 6:10, we hear the first question:"How long, Lord?" In Revelation 6:17, we hear the second question: "Who can stand?" The answers to these questions will help us endure.

"How Long, O Lord?"

If you've ever lived through difficult times, you know that time does not fly when you're not having fun. Suffering seems to slow the clock, and trials are always long and hard. In the midst of pain, we all ask, "How long? Will this go on forever? When will it end?"

As a child of the '80s, I watched every single *Rocky* movie . . . all 27 of them. I loved those movies—underdog athlete overcoming odds to reach prize—and my favorite part in each was the "training montage." Do you remember the original movie? Rocky Balboa wants to go the distance with heavyweight champ Apollo Creed. So as the theme music *Gonna Fly Now* builds, in a quick sequence of scenes, we see Rocky jogging through the streets of Philadelphia, doing one handed push-ups, training with a speed bag, and dancing around a freezing meat locker punching a side of beef. His speed and agility improve, building to the climax when he sprints up the Art Museum steps to look over the city and lift his arms in the classic Rocky pose. Watching as a kid, I got goosebumps.

Someday when I visit Philadelphia, I am so going to do that.

The point of the training montage is clear: Rocky is paying his dues to become a champ. That's essential—great struggles make great stories. Nobody goes to see a movie with the plotline:"naturally gifted athlete does nothing particularly demanding in preparation and easily wins title."[4]

But the deception of the training montage is this: it seems as if the trials before the triumph are relatively brief. Those 2-3 inspirational minutes in the movie are actually 2-3 hard months in real life for Rocky. The montage collapses grueling weeks of training into about 120 upbeat seconds.

---

4. Jeff Manion, *The Land Between* (Grand Rapids: Zondervan, 2010) 177.

If you're living through hard times, they don't feel like 120 upbeat seconds.

Living In the Training Montage

I've lived through some difficult times. Two years ago, a massive EF-5 tornado tore through our city of Joplin, Missouri—the deadliest U.S. tornado in the last 65 years. By God's grace, a falling tree saved my family and me from driving straight into the rain-wrapped funnel cloud, but the devastation was staggering. Eight thousand homes destroyed, four hundred businesses gone, thousands injured, 161 lives lost. We lost three friends from our church, a student from the Bible college, and a retired faculty member. Dozens of friends lost their homes.

In the two years since, we've lived in the training montage.

As we've tried to put our community back together, we've all pushed through challenge after challenge, blood, sweat, and tears. We've seen our city reach deep and dig out. We've helped families grieve their loss, heal their wounds, rebuild their homes and restart their lives.

Because it's been a great struggle, it makes a great story—underdog city overcoming odds to rebuild better than ever—and I can testify that Joplin is stronger for it. Someday if they make a movie of Joplin's story, the director might decide to edit these 2 years of rebuilding down to 2 inspirational minutes with cool upbeat music.

But actually living them?

That has been long and hard.

The persecuted believers of Asia Minor are feeling that. They are weary of their woe, and they hear their own question echoed when the saints of the sixth seal cry out, "How long?" The saints there are told to "wait a little longer, until the number of their fellow servants and brothers who were to be killed as they had been was completed" (Rev 6:11). The word "completed" hints at an important truth: the martyrdom of the saints, while tragic and wrong, is still under God's watchful eye.

To be clear, he is not causing this persecution—that's the work of evil men—but God is not unmindful of it either. God will not allow the suffering to go on forever; a time will come when he will say "enough."

As Warren Wiersbe puts it, "When you are in the furnace, the Father keeps His hand on the thermostat and His eye on the clock. He knows just how much you can take."

That's good news for the early believers ... and for us. When we know that suffering cannot endure past its appointed time, we can endure more patiently.

"Grace Withereth Without Adversity"

By the way, deceptive as its timeframe is, a training montage does remind us: suffering can have a purpose. For Rocky, his pain brought gain; he became a better boxer. Notice what the martyred saints gain from their troubles: "a white robe" (Rev 6:11). The white robes are symbols of blessedness and purity, and we are reminded that God uses suffering to purify us.

Like a boxer, the grueling challenges we face strengthen our spiritual muscles. "Consider it pure joy, my brothers, whenever you face trials of many kinds, because you know that the testing of your faith develops perseverance" (Jas 1:2-3).

Of course, if we are not wise, we can allow suffering to make us bitter instead of better. Bishop Fulton Sheen once exclaimed, "Think of how much suffering goes to waste!" When we experience trials, if all we do is simply grit our teeth and bear it, we may not come out on the other side with purer faith—just ground-down molars.

"Patient endurance" (Rev 1:9) means that we actually allow God to mold us, stretch us, and work his will in us through the hard times. God often teaches his greatest lessons in the school of suffering, and much as we wish we could live pain-free lives, we would be the poorer for it.

As the old Scottish preacher Samuel Rutherford put it, "The greatest temptation out of hell is to live without temptation. Grace withereth without adversity. The devil is but God's master fencer, to teach us to handle our weapons."

"How long?" The answer to that question is not a timetable, but two simple, needed truths. First, when we suffer, no matter how long, God will not let it go too long. His eye is on the clock. Second, when we suffer, we are being prepared for a "white robe." We're living in the training montage.

If those two things are true, is it possible that we could find our song again?

"Who Can Stand?"

In the fifth seal, the martyrs ask, "How long?" But the question in the sixth seal comes from a very different group of people. When the cataclysmic events of this seal are unleashed, everyone else on earth—from the most powerful to the least—runs to the hills to hide. They have seen nothing like this before! This seal has likely brought us to the end of the world, and these catastrophes picture God's final, fiery judgment.

God's judgment at the end of time will not be fickle or impulsive—he has waited patiently and he will be perfectly just—but his judgment will be a terrifying thing to behold. "We sometimes say, in seasons of havoc and terror, that all hell is breaking loose. But that's nothing. What is truly terrible is when all *heaven* breaks loose!"[5]

Indeed, these unrepentant sinners call out for the rocks to fall on them and hide them from the face of God and of the Lamb. It is then that they ask, in utter hopelessness, "For the great day of their wrath has come, and who can stand?"

Answer: No one.

Except . . .

In Revelation 7, John's readers are given two parallel visions with one purpose: to reassure them that they are kept securely in the hand of God. Who can stand safely in the face of God's judgment? Answer: They can.

God Is Good At Math

In the first vision, John sees a group of God's servants—144,000 of them, 12,000 from each of Israel's 12 tribes. Who are these people? Most likely they simply represent the complete company of the people of God. The twelve tribes symbolize the new Israel, which is the church (Rom 9:6). The number twelve communicates completeness, and the number one thousand communicates vastness. So twelve times one thousand times twelve tribes (144,000) equals the vast and complete people of God.

By the way, notice that it's not 143,999. Not one of the redeemed is missing.

---

5. Mark Buchanan, *The Holy Wild* (Sisters: Multnomah, 2003) 98.

My 17-year-old daughter Lydia is a jokester and a quick wit. Someone once asked her to describe herself in three words. She smiled slyly and counted off the words on her fingers, "I'm bad at math."

God is not bad at math, and his count is always accurate. When a good shepherd with 100 sheep only counts 99, he does not rest until he finds the last one and brings it safely home. God never leaves a sheep behind, and not one of the 144,000 will be forgotten. Each has been sealed with the King's signet as his property, and while their bodies may still suffer, their souls are safe.

A News Flash From the Near Future

John is given a second vision in Revelation 7:9-17, parallel to the first. It is still a vision of God's redeemed people, but the emphases in each vision are different:

- The first is God's people in the present; the second is God's people in the future.
- The first is God's people symbolized by the number 144,000; the second is God's people as they truly are—"a great multitude that no one can count."
- The first portrays God's people figuratively as true Israel; the second shows us that God's people are literally from "every nation, tribe, people and language."
- The first pictures their security while on earth; the second pictures their salvation someday in heaven.

What a salvation it is! With this glimpse into the future, John sees the redeemed standing before God's throne wearing white robes and holding palm branches—a symbol of victory. They were faithful in the middle of the story, so they are victorious in the end!

Now they enjoy the blessedness of heaven: constant personal access to God, no more hunger, no more thirst, no more suffering, no more tears, only rest and peace and security and refreshment (Rev 7:15-17).

This vision is meant to remind John's readers that, in light of eternity, we are wise to endure. "Suffering," said one wise old German monk, "is a short pain and a long joy." The apostle Paul wrote, "Therefore we do not lose heart ... for our light and momentary troubles are achieving for us an eternal glory that far outweighs them all" (2 Cor 4:16-17).

Phillip Yancey tells the story of some Americans in a World War II German prison camp who, unbeknownst to the guards, built a makeshift radio. One day news came over the radio that the German high command had surrendered, ending the war, but because of a communications breakdown, the German guards didn't yet know. It wasn't until four days later that the Americans woke to find the Germans had fled, leaving the gates unlocked.

In the three interim days, those prisoners still suffered. They were still mocked, still abused, but they were changed. They waved to the guards, laughed at the German Shepherd dogs, told jokes over meals, and in the midst of their captivity, they sang.

Why? Because they knew their salvation was sure and soon.

In Revelation 7, the oppressed believers get a news bulletin about the near future. The time is coming when they will stand before the throne. The Lamb will be their shepherd and lead them to springs of living water, and God will wipe every tear from their eyes.

Their salvation is sure and soon, so they can endure patiently.

And they can sing.

Their song is in 7:10, "Salvation belongs to our God." Composer Wilfrid Mellers once said, "Where there is music, there is hope." The ragtag believers of Asia Minor have been given hope, and now it finds voice in song.

If you are going through hard times, like Chippy the parakeet, then hear the message of Revelation 7: Heaven awaits and God has not forgotten you. There is hope.

Endure patiently.

And sing.

DISSCUSSION QUESTIONS
Chapter 7
Endure Suffering Patiently

1. Has anyone ever asked you why God allows suffering in the world? How did you respond? Have you yourself ever asked, "How long?"

2. What evidence of the four horsemen and other cosmic turmoil do you see around you in the world today?

3. What valuable lessons in life have you learned in the school of suffering?.

4. While God's seal doesn't protect our body, it does protect our soul and "baptizes our pain in hope." How does a vision of heaven help you through life's trials here on earth?

8

CHAPTER EIGHT
BEAR WITNESS BOLDLY
Revelation 8-11

"When one preaches Christianity in such a way that the echo answers, 'Away with that man, he does not deserve to live,' know that this is the Christianity of the New Testament."
—Soren Kierkegaard—

I laughed when I saw the bumper sticker. It read: "Jesus is coming! Look busy."

Not bad advice.

The Bible teaches that a day is coming when the trumpet of the archangel will sound, the eastern sky will split and Jesus will come riding back to earth on the clouds, followed by his angel armies. History will end, and all humanity will be judged — some to enjoy God's presence forever and others to eternal torment (Matt 24:27ff; 25:31ff).

We know that Christ's return will be *unexpected and without warning*, like a thief in the night (1 Thess 5:1-2). We also know that his return will be *soon* (Rev 22:7,12,20). All the prophecies to be fulfilled before his second coming have already taken place, and there is nothing to prevent Jesus from crashing back through the clouds before you finish reading this sentence. I have a friend who keeps a sign on his office door: "Perhaps Today." Every morning, he is reminded that the Lord could return that very day.

Jesus is coming. Look busy.

What Will He Catch You Doing?

Here's a multiple choice question: If Jesus returned today, what would you like him to catch you doing?

a. *Praying.* You're at a church picnic, eyes closed, praying for the food, "Dear Lord . . ." Suddenly you hear a voice from above: "Yes?" You open your eyes and see Jesus descending into your picnic!

b. *Worshipping.* Your church is singing *When the Roll Is Called Up Yonder* on a Sunday morning: "When the trumpet of the Lord shall sound . . ." Suddenly the actual sound of the archangel's trumpet pierces the church walls. The roof peels back, and the whole congregation ascends toward Jesus — still singing!

c. *Watching American Idol.* (Hint: wrong answer)

d. *Baptizing.* You're standing in the baptistery with someone you led to Christ, saying those familiar words as you immerse your friend: "Buried with him in death and raised with him in new life." Suddenly, right when you say "raised," you both actually start rising up out of the water and into the sky to meet Jesus!

I think my answer would be letter "d." In light of Christ's imminent return, what should we be busy doing? Listen to the last verse of *When the Roll Is Called Up Yonder*: "Let us labor for the Master from the dawn till setting sun. Let us talk of all His wondrous love and care." Our work is to witness.

In 2 Timothy 4, Paul put it this way, "In the presence of God and of Christ who will judge the living and the dead, and in view of his appearing and his kingdom, I give you this charge: Preach the Word." In view of Christ's quickly approaching appearance, we must labor diligently now to take God's Word to the world. Let him catch us evangelizing.

Jesus is coming. Look busy.

The Sound Of Seven Trumpets

That is the message of Revelation 8-11.

Here we come to the second of the three sets of seven judgments (seals, trumpets, bowls). In our discussion of Revelation's structure back in chapter 3, we mentioned the concept of "progressive parallelism." The idea is simply this: each of the three "sevens of judgments" is narrating the same sequence of events (not three different sequences). It's telling the same story three times, with a little more intensity each time, and the story is of God's judgments throughout history that lead up to the end of the world.

So in Revelation 8-11, the seven trumpets (blown by seven angels) will sound a bit like a rerun of the seven seals in Revelation 6-7.

Remember VHS? After the seventh seal has us in heaven at the end of time, we "rewind the tape" and, with the first trumpet, start back on earth in a time of suffering.

This time around, however, the story ramps up.

When the first four trumpets are blown, suffering ensues just as it did with the first four seals. But instead of one-fourth of the earth being affected, this time it's one-third. One third of the earth, trees, grass, sea, sea creatures, ships, rivers, sun, moon, and stars feel the heat of God's wrath. God has turned up the power on his judgment, moving the dial from 25% to 33%.

But do not take this as a sign of God's increasing hostility. This is an act of mercy. "He is patient . . . not wanting anyone to perish, but everyone to come to repentance" (2 Pet 3:9). Given the stubborn rebellion of human hearts, God would have every right to turn the judgment dial to 100% and wipe mankind out in its entirety. But he doesn't.

No, God instead brings (just) judgment on a minority, in the hope that the majority will take heed and repent. He is turning up the heat to get their attention. When Israel rebelled in the wilderness, God's righteous judgment consumed some on the outskirts of the camp—but not the whole encampment—prompting the people to repent (Num 11:1-2). Mercy stayed God's hand from greater destruction, and his judgment was a warning, calling people to turn from their wicked ways.

Unheeded Warnings

In fact, after the first four trumpets unleash the elemental forces of nature, God issues another warning (with an eagle!), because the trumpets to follow will instead unleash the demonic forces of hell itself. Without exegeting every detail of these next two trumpets, we will notice this: they combine to describe a vast, devouring force of invading horsemen with long hair coming from the east. (The river Euphrates was the Roman Empire's eastern border.)

Upon hearing this, John's readers would've immediately thought, "Parthians!" These fierce barbaric warriors on Rome's eastern frontier wore long hair, were renowned horsemen, and a generation earlier had actually won an unprecedented victory over a Roman army— unnerving the Empire and creating fear of invasion. The demonic forces in Revelation 9 are painted in the likeness of Rome's most dreaded threat.

What is going on with all this weird imagery?

Very simply, God is warning the people of earth that, if they do not repent, very bad things will happen. It is no accident that this second set of seven judgments is symbolized by trumpets. Throughout Scripture, trumpets signaled that something momentous was coming: a king's entrance, an army's attack, even a divine rescue. Trumpets were warnings, and the message of a trumpet blast was, "Make yourself ready!"

A preacher and youth minister had just finished pounding a large sign in the church's front yard which read, "Turn now or perish." A passing driver shook his fist at the pair and yelled, "Keep it to yourself, you religious zealots!" A moment later, the two heard the sounds of a tremendous car crash. The youth minister turned to the preacher and said, "I told you we should have just written 'Bridge out ahead.'"

Unheeded warnings, of course, are no laughing matter, and God's judgment is serious business. The trumpeted chaos pictured here is to prompt people to prepare their souls for eternity. Sadly, they do not heed the warnings. "The rest of mankind that were not killed by these plagues still did not repent" (Rev 9:20).

Missionaries Cleverly Disguised

In each cycle of seven judgments (seals, trumpets, bowls), there is an interlude between the sixth and seventh. The pause between the sixth and seventh seal reminded the saints of their security. But here, the pause between the sixth and seventh trumpet — Revelation 10 and 11 — reminds the saints of their responsibility to witness. The previous six trumpets pictured a terrible lost world and a terrible coming judgment; someone must speak up, someone must warn, someone must call the world to repentance and point them to salvation.

Who is that someone? It's the church.

Revelation 10 and 11 include more details than we can explore here, but let's get the big picture. First, notice the main characters: John (Rev 10) and the two witnesses (Rev 11). Second, notice their activity: all three are commanded to speak the message of God.

Who exactly are the two witnesses? Answer: we don't know for sure. But we've got some clues. They're called "the two olive trees and the two lampstands" (Rev 11:4). The olive tree symbolized Israel, the Old Testament people of God, while the lampstand pictured the church, the

New Testament people of God. They have the power of Moses "to turn the waters into blood" and the power of Elijah "to shut up the sky" (Rev 11:6).[1] Could this refer to the church having the power of God's Word in the Law (Moses) and the Prophets (Elijah)? We don't know, but it certainly does tell us that God's servants in the church have the same access to God's power as his servants of old.

If I was guessing, I'd say the two witnesses represent the Spirit-empowered church of God.

What is that power to be used for? To proclaim God's truth. We the church are called to speak God's message to the world. Too often, the American church wants to delegate that task to its hired personnel—the preachers and ministers—and is content to sit on the sidelines cheering them on. The old comedian Flip Wilson once quipped, "I'm a Jehovah's Bystander. They invited me to be a Witness, but I didn't want to get involved." Too many contemporary Christians have declined God's invitation to witness.

The fact is: it's not an invitation. It's a command—the last one Jesus gave before he ascended to heaven (Matt 28:18-20). The Great Commission was not just for the apostles, but for all believers, and if you are a Christian, you are called to be an evangelist. You got into the ministry when you got out of the baptistery, and you must see yourself as a witness. I like the lady who, when asked about her job, said, "Oh, I'm a missionary . . . cleverly disguised as a grocery store clerk."

In a lost world, no matter our vocation, we are all missionaries.

Jesus is coming. Look busy.

Witness From God's Word

What exactly does Revelation 10-11 tell us about this call to witness? At least these three things: we are to witness *from God's Word*, witness *through hard suffering*, and witness *with great urgency*.

In Revelation 10, an angel gives John a scroll and tells him to eat it. Immediately we know this scroll is the Word of God (or at least a portion of it), because we remember Ezekiel eating the scroll of Scripture.[2] John, just like Ezekiel, says it tasted like honey.

God's Word is sweet, and to a hungry world, the good news of God's grace is a welcome taste. When we witness, we are always wise to point people straight to the Bible. Scripture has transforming power.

---

1. See Exodus 7:20 and 1 Kings 17:1.
2. Ezekiel 3:3

I'll tell you when I'm reminded of this the most: when I'm preaching a bad sermon. It happens to all preachers. Despite our best effort, we end up doing a homiletical belly flop. (I have a friend who preached a clunker one Sunday. As he shook hands at the door after worship, the kind church folks all said, "Nice sermon. Nice job. Nice sermon." But one honest older lady said, "Nice try.") During my "nice try" sermons, I just want to get done quickly, go home and try to do better next week.

But God, in his great sense of humor, sometimes gives me the best response to my worst sermons—just to remind me it's not about me. As the invitation hymn is sung, people are coming down the aisle! Decisions are being made. A lady is shaking my hand, saying, "You have no idea how that touched me."

I'm thinking, "You're right. I have no idea how that touched you."

The fact is, however, I do know. Ineffective as *my* words may have been, if I've been faithful to Scripture, *God's* Word is still divinely effective. In Isaiah 55:11, God says, "My word that goes out from my mouth . . . will not return to me empty, but will accomplish what I desire and achieve the purpose for which I sent it." Hebrews 4:12 says, "For the word of God is living and active. Sharper than any double-edged sword, it penetrates even to dividing soul and spirit, joints and marrow; it judges the thoughts and attitudes of the heart."

When you witness to a lost world, give them the sweet, life-changing power of God's Word.

Witness Through Hard Suffering

When John tastes the scroll, it is sweet, but when he swallows God's message, it is bitter (10:10). That's because not everyone likes to hear the truth. Karl Marx said religion was the opiate of the masses, a sedative to make them feel better. But as Tim Keller puts it, "Christianity is by no means the opiate of the people. It's more like the smelling salts."[3] The gospel rouses those who hear it from their self-centered dream and awakens them to the bracing reality of their sinfulness. But just as smelling salts are hard to take, God's truth is not always welcome. As someone said, "If you try to be the light of the world, you're going to attract a few bugs."

3. Tim Keller, *The Prodigal God* (New York: Dutton, 2008), 113.

Just ask the two witnesses in Revelation 11. When they finish their testimony, they are attacked and killed. Read through your Bible, and you realize that God's messengers should probably get hazard pay. Prophets have always had a high mortality rate, and you wouldn't want to insure an apostle. They pretty much all end up dead prematurely for preaching God's truth.

When we faithfully proclaim God's message, we too will face hostility. Sometimes, in the interest of keeping the peace, we can be tempted to keep silent. Nobody wants to be seen as intolerant or judgmental. It's easier to just be quiet. But as one African-American preacher put it, "The church must be prophetic, or it will be pathetic."

Which is why I need these chapters in Revelation. Notice: John doesn't write as much to instruct us *in* witnessing as much as to inspire us *to* witnessing. I don't need more explanation. I need examples. It's not information I lack. It's courage.

Richard Wurmbrand was a pastor in Romania behind the Iron Curtain, arrested in 1948 and tortured for 14 years because of his faith in Christ. In his book *Tortured for Christ*, he wrote, "It was strictly forbidden to preach to other prisoners . . . It was understood that whoever was caught doing this received a severe beating. But a number of us decided to pay the price for the privilege of preaching, so we accepted their terms. It was a deal: we preached and they beat us. We were happy preaching; they were happy beating us — so everyone was happy."[4]

Wow. When I read that story, I am inspired to witness no matter what small suffering I may endure, and seeing the two witnesses in Revelation speak boldly for God stiffens my spine as well. Their preaching is courageous, and their example is contagious. If they paid the price for faithfulness, surely I can speak up for Christ to my neighbor. Though the world may reject, God will reward (11:18).

Witness With Great Urgency

In 11:11, God miraculously raises the two witnesses from the dead, perhaps picturing our own resurrection at the end of time, because when the seventh trumpet blows we are brought to the end of the world. Christ's kingdom has arrived, and "the time has come for judging the dead" (11:18).

---

4. Richard Wurmbrand, *Tortured for Christ* (London: Hodder and Stoughton, 1970) 41.

We have been given notice: the time for our witness is short. The very next blast of the trumpet will be Jesus' return, so we must speak God's message with great urgency. We must have the attitude of the great preacher George Whitefield who said, "God forbid that I should travel with anybody a quarter of an hour without speaking of Christ to them."

In his autobiography *Just As I Am*, Billy Graham told of a golf outing with President Kennedy, a less-than-faithful Catholic. Kennedy asked Mr. Graham if he believed in the Second Coming of Jesus Christ. When Billy said he most certainly did, Kennedy asked, "Well, does my church believe it?" Mr. Graham said it was in the Catholic Church's creeds, to which President Kennedy replied, "They don't preach it. They don't tell us much about it. I'd like to know what you think."

After Billy explained what the Bible said about Christ's return, Kennedy replied, "Very interesting. You've given me a lot to think about. We'll have to talk more about that someday." Here is Billy's conclusion to the story:

> The last time I was with Kennedy was at the 1963 National Prayer Breakfast. I had the flu. After we both gave our talks, we walked out of the hotel to his car together. At the curb, he turned to me. "Billy, could you ride back to the White House with me? I'd like to talk with you for a minute."
>
> "Mr. President, I've got a fever," I protested. "I don't want to give you this thing. Couldn't we wait and talk some other time?" It was a cold, snowy day, and I was freezing as I stood there without my overcoat. "Of course," he said graciously.[5]

Then came November 22, 1963, and Billy Graham never saw President Kennedy alive again. Reflecting back, he writes, "His hesitation at the car door, and his request, haunt me still. What was on his mind? Should I have gone with him? It was an irrecoverable moment."[6]

The truth is: we do not know when our unsaved friends will stand before the judgment seat of Christ. We have seen, with each trumpet blast, the terrible judgment they will face outside the gospel, so we must "make the most of every opportunity" (Col 4:5).

When you see a conversational opening to give a word of witness, take it. It may be "an irrecoverable moment." Witness from God's Word, through hard suffering and with great urgency.

Jesus is coming. Look busy.

---

5. Billy Graham, *Just As I Am* (San Francisco: Harper Collins, 1997) 472-473.
6. *Ibid.*, 473.

Disscussion Questions
Chapter 8
Bear Witness Boldley

1. How often do you think about the reality of hell? If you pictured your neighbors experiencig God's judgment, how might it affect your witness?

2. Why is witnessing sometimes hard? How does our culture react to the gospel message? Have you ever experienced hostility when bearing witness?

3. What can help us overcome our own reluctance to witness? Who are your examples of courageous witness?

4. Who in your sphere of influence needs to hear about Jesus? What is a specific way you can share the message of Christ with them in the next month?

CHAPTER NINE
SEE EVIL CLEARLY
Revelation 12-14

*"The world is not a playground, but a battleground.
We are not here to frolic. We are here to fight."*
—A. W. Tozer—

A blind man walks into a barbershop, and as the barber begins to cut his hair, the blind man says, "I just heard the best blonde joke ever—"

The barber interrupts, "Listen, buddy, I understand you're blind, so I'll cut you some slack. But you need to know: I'm a Golden Gloves boxer, and I'm blonde. The barber to your right is a former Navy Seal, and he's blonde. The barber to your left is a former NFL linebacker, and he's blonde."

"To top it off," says the barber, "the guy at the cash register is a black belt in karate, and he's blonde. Do you still wanna tell that joke?"

"Nah," says the blind man. "I don't want to have to explain it four times."

It can be dangerous when you don't see your enemy clearly.

The Masquerade Is Over

If there's one thing the devil wants to do, it's to keep you from seeing him at all—or at least, his true identity. The apostle Paul tells us that "Satan himself masquerades as an angel of light" (2 Cor 11:14). Our enemy is clever, and he knows that if we saw him unmasked, we would recoil in dread at the sight of true evil. So the devil has chosen to wage a campaign of subterfuge, an undercover operation rather than open assault. His disguise is beautiful, his words soothing, his demeanor pleasant.

But in Revelation 12-14, John rips back the veil on the spiritual realm, and we suddenly see Satan as he truly is. The angel of light is unmasked, and in its place, we see a horrifying, violent dragon. Huge and blood-red, this grotesque dragon spreads his leathery wings, malice dripping from jagged teeth, and sears his enemies with fiery, sulfurous breath.

Instinctively, we shrink back in revulsion. There is nothing subtle here. Upon seeing this image, even a child would recognize: this dragon is wicked.

One December, my wife and I gathered our children in the living room so I could tell them the Christmas story. On the table, I set out a nativity set—cute little bathrobe figures with smiling faces. They settled in to hear the heartwarming, familiar story.

Until I put a dragon in the middle of the manger scene.

The snarling red figure towered over the tiny happy-faced Joseph and Mary and baby Jesus. My kids' eyes suddenly widened. What was this? An evil monster in the lovable nativity? The scene that looked like Norman Rockwell suddenly felt like Stephen King. What did it mean?

Then I told the Christmas story from Revelation 12.

Behind the Scenes At Christmas

In Revelation 12, we sense a shift in the book. For the past six chapters, we've watched mayhem on the earth, but now the camera pans upward to the heavens. We discover that, behind the conflict on our smaller visible world, there is a battle raging in an invisible world as large as the cosmos itself.

We start by peering behind-the-scenes at Christmas. In Revelation 12, John suddenly sees "a great and wondrous sign" in heaven—a large, pregnant woman wearing a crown of twelve stars, preparing to give birth to "a son, a male child, who will rule all the nations with an iron scepter" (Rev 12:5). The baby, described here with language from Psalm 2:9, is the Messiah. Who is the lady? She's too big to be little Mary. The twelve stars likely refer to the twelve Hebrew tribes (Gen 37:9). She is Israel, the Messiah's mother nation.

So we are at the nativity, Christ soon to be born. But suddenly a great red dragon appears—so large his tail sweeps a third of the stars from the heavens—bent on killing the almost-born child. "The reptile is a crimson gash, violating the sky," and we cringe, anticipating the baby's bloody, violent end.[1] The child is born, the dragon lunges, we hold our breath . . . and at the last possible moment, the child is rescued by God!

---

1. Peterson, *Thunder*, 120.

In the living room with my kids that December, I explained. It wasn't just King Herod trying to kill the baby Jesus; it was the devil himself. Praise God that Jesus was protected! But when the dragon can't kill the baby boy and is thrown out of heaven by Michael the archangel, Satan turns to devour the woman. God miraculously rescues the woman too, so finally in frustrated fury, the dragon attacks the woman's offspring.

I told my kids: that's us. The church is the offspring of God's Old Testament people. We are the descendants of the woman Israel, and that means we are square in the devil's crosshairs. The scene vividly pictures this truth: we have an unseen Enemy bent on our destruction. Revelation 12 graphically depicts Satan's malice. "He longs to drink the blood and eat the flesh" of God's people and "craves the terror of your children."[2] This is serious business.

A Song In Our Throats and a Sword In Our Hands

We must never forget that we are at war. The Christmas story is not a "religious glow to warm a dark night," and Revelation 12 reminds us that we can't sentimentalize the nativity.[3] It is not just a cute little scene with shepherds and wise men; a dragon lurks outside the stable. The birth of Jesus was not just meant to inspire a cozy Christmas carol sing with hot chocolate in our hands. It inspired a great war across the heavens, and now we are part of that battle.

How shall we respond? We must walk out the stable door "with, as one psalmist put it, high praises of God in our throats and two-edged swords in our hands (Ps 149:6)."[4] By all means, let us sing the Christmas carols, thanking God for the gift of His Son. But let us also be armed and on our guard against the dragon.

As a kid, I loved *The Hobbit*, J. R. R. Tolkien's story of a little fellow named Bilbo Baggins who helps a remnant of dwarves reclaim their mountain home. The only problem: a deadly dragon named Smaug now inhabits the mountain, so they must not blithely walk back in to their old home unawares. As Tolkien writes, "It does not do to leave a live dragon out of your calculations, if you live near him."[5]

2. Peter Hiett, *Eternity Now* (Nashville: Integrity, 2003) 164.
3. *Ibid.*, 117.
4. *Ibid.*, 122.
5. J. R. R. Tolkien, *The Hobbit* (Boston: Houghton Mifflin, 1966) 123.

The fact is: we live near the dragon. Thrown from heaven, he now prowls the earth, and if we want to stay faithful, we must watch carefully for his attacks. The apostle Paul warned that we must not let "Satan... outwit us, for we are not unaware of his schemes" (2 Cor 2:11). So how exactly *will* the devil seek to devour us? What are his schemes?

Satan is not the equal opposite of God. He is not the "dark side of the force," with all the same powers as the "light side," only used for evil. While formidably powerful, he is not omnipresent like God. He cannot be everywhere, so Satan, as a cunning and intelligent schemer, has devised a strategy to leverage his influence for the largest maximum impact worldwide.

Specifically, Satan targets societal structures—institutions which hold great sway over vast numbers of people. If he can corrupt the smaller number of people who control such cultural structures, then the institutions themselves will do his work for him in the lives of thousands or even millions of people. He does not have to target each person individually. If the devil can simply infect the political or religious or economic "bloodstream" of a culture, then the virus will spread throughout the entire system. It is a wickedly brilliant plan.

Starting in Revelation 13, John helps us factor the dragon into our "calculations" by showing us three such schemes of the devil—*godless government, false religion,* and *hedonistic culture.* He is writing to say: keep your eyes open.

Satan Uses Godless Government

Reading Revelation, we see that the dragon enlists three allies in his offensive against believers: two grotesque beasts and a gaudy, lewd prostitute. (With these images, John is again unmasking evil so we can see that what looks harmless is really hellish and repulsive.) What do these three figures represent? Each is a societal structure Satan uses.

The first beast is *godless government,* with its goal of physical persecution. The second beast is *false religion,* with its goal of intellectual deception. The prostitute is *hedonistic culture,* with its goal of moral corruption. While Satan has used these three allies during many eras and in many places, here in Revelation they are "symbols of the Roman empire ... namely Rome the persecutor, Rome the deceiver and Rome the seducer."[6]

---

6. John Stott, *The Cross of Christ* (Downer's Grove: IVP, 1986) 248.

The first structure Satan co-opts, then, is government. In Revelation 13, the dragon brings forth a beast out of the sea which looks suspiciously like him — both have seven heads and ten horns. This beast has what appears to be a fatal head wound, but which has now healed — most likely a reference to Nero. (He died of a self-inflicted head wound, but a *Nero Redivivus* myth persisted that he would someday come back to life.) By referencing a notoriously anti-Christian emperor, John's point is simply that this first beast represents the godless Roman government.

The important details: the beast demands worship and utters blasphemies, just like Emperor Domitian demanded worship and declared himself "Lord and God." When believers do not participate in the imperial cult, the beast then "makes war against the saints" (Rev 13:7).

Of course, this refers to the physical persecution John's readers are enduring at the bloody hands of Rome. But this beast symbolizes any godless, oppressive government that exalts itself above Christ. In Uganda, over 400,000 Christians were persecuted by Idi Amin, and in the atheistic former U.S.S.R., believers were systematically beaten and imprisoned. Think of modern-day Cuba, China, India and Muslim countries like the Sudan.

I love America. I'm grateful for our freedoms, cherish our heritage, and have a whole shelf of books on Washington, Jefferson, Madison and Lincoln. I was born on an Army base, appreciate the sacrifice of our servicemen, respect the office of President, and salute the flag. Call me corny, but I can get misty-eyed at *The Star Spangled Banner*. I even own the movie *Captain America!* Patriotism is not a bad word in my book.

But John's warning is: open your eyes. Roman citizens — even Christian ones — were likely proud of their country. They were the premier power in the world, with an unmatched military, unprecedented freedoms, and unparalleled economic opportunities. To her citizens, Roman patriotism didn't feel wrong, and respecting the Emperor seemed like a right and proper thing . But John says, because this government opposes Christ, it is a grotesque beast.

Which means I can never blindly give America my loyalty. I live in a nation that censors the Bible in school, passes out free condoms to children, and kills more unborn babies every year than American lives lost in all our wars combined. A nation where marriage is no longer between one man and woman. A nation that seems increasingly hostile to Biblical faith.

I still pledge allegiance to the flag, but never before I pledge allegiance to the cross.

The dragon stalks us. Keep your eyes open.

Satan Uses False Religion

Yesterday I talked to my son in Africa. Nineteen-year-old Luke is on a summer internship with missionaries in a predominantly Muslim Saharan country. He's 60 miles from a terrorist attack that just occurred, working in 130-degree heat, one of five white guys in a radius of 200 miles, trying to grow crops in the desert and build agricultural equipment out of literally almost nothing.

He's loving every minute of it.

Luke's a hardworking farm kid, but mostly he's a bike-ramping, bungee-jumping, cliff-diving adrenaline junkie who craves adventure—the harder the better. He and his cousin once chopped ice out of a lake to go waterskiing in 38 degree water. (Hypothermia sets in at eight minutes; they skied for six.) He's always up for a challenge. He's a happy, relational person who loves making friends and pulling pranks.

But yesterday in our videochat, he was in tears.

During the month Luke's spent there, the people have captured his heart. Village kids flock to wrestle with him, and with the missionary's help, he sits in the afternoon shade talking with the village men. He's even had several fathers offer their daughters in marriage! (I told him to just bring back souvenirs instead.) Luke knows their names, their stories, their personalities—who's a jokester, who's earnest, who's hurting. They've talked about Jesus; Luke even used a picture book to tell the story. He wants desperately for his new friends to know Christ.

But the iron grip of Islam holds them captive.

So tears streamed down his face yesterday. "I know it's a metaphor, Dad," said Luke, his voice breaking, "but there really is no light in their eyes. Islam is all about fear, and there's no joy. There's no music here, no hope. Their lives are empty. I want them to know Jesus so much, so much. Pray for them, Dad. Please pray." His heart was broken for his friends Lagri, Mairu, Shatima, Maman and all the people of the village, lost in their religion.

The second beast is indeed a monster.

In Revelation 13, Satan co-opts a second societal structure—false religion. John pictures it as a second beast, coming out of the earth. He has "two horns like a lamb," (trying to imitate the true Lamb), performs miraculous signs, and promotes worship of the first beast. If the first beast's power was persecution, the second beast's power is deception. He "deceived the inhabitants of the earth" (Rev 13:14) and is called "the false prophet" (Rev 19:20). For John's readers, the imperial cult and the Roman pantheon of gods were the work of the second beast.

This beast remains a powerful ally, because Satan uses false religions to enslave billions of people through deceptive systems like Islam, Hinduism, Buddhism, Mormonism, animism, the occult, and secular humanism. Any false philosophy is his tool.

He is the father of lies, and instead of physically attacking these people, he wages a war of propaganda. They are his if he can just get them to believe falsehood: "you can earn your way to heaven," "all religions lead to the same place," "there is no God," "God doesn't love you and could never forgive you," "God just wants you to be happy."

His whispering voice lies behind all the deceiving philosophies of the world.[7]

The dragon stalks us. Keep your eyes open.

Satan Uses Hedonistic Culture

Satan's third ally is mentioned in Revelation 14:8, "Fallen is Babylon the Great, which made all the nations drink the maddening wine of her adulteries." But she's not fully introduced until Revelation 17:1 where she's called the "great prostitute." There we discover that this prostitute is Rome herself—"the great city that rules over the kings of the earth" and that sits on "seven hills," as Rome did (Rev 17:9-18).

The prostitute represents Rome's hedonistic culture—another societal structure Satan uses. This prostitute gives herself to succeeding in business (Rev 18:23), acquiring luxuries (Rev 18:3), drinking (Rev 18:6), pursuing sexual pleasure (Rev 17:2), and attaining power and fame (Rev 18:7). She's all about herself, and she wants to entice John's readers to think only about themselves.

---

7. We aren't to receive the "mark of the beast" (Rev 13:16-18). What does this mean? Simply, the word "beast" in alphanumeric code is 666—"man's number" because it imperfectly falls short of God's perfect 777. The point: don't be marked by fallen mankind's behaviors ("right hand") or thinking ("forehead"). Be marked by God's way of thinking (Rev 14:1). You'll be outcast on earth ("no buying or selling") but welcome in heaven.

If the first beast uses power to physically persecute, and the second beast uses propaganda to intellectually deceive, then the prostitute uses temptation to morally corrupt. The culture around us—a society's collective habits of education, art, music, economic activity, entertainment and social interaction—unconsciously shapes us every day. Through the prostitute, Satan seeks to gradually seduce us into increasingly selfish, pleasure-seeking, goodness-corrupting habits. If greed and sexual promiscuity and lack of courtesy and crude humor become the cultural norms, he wins.

Right now, in our culture, the score is in his favor.

Growing up in the '80s, we watched *The Cosby Show*, a clean program with strong values. Today the networks offer us *The Family Guy* with a foul-mouthed, sexually crude baby. We didn't go from A to Z overnight. The culture guardians incrementally lowered the bar over time, seducing us with slightly more risqué laughs at each step. "The safest road to hell," wrote C. S. Lewis, "is the gradual one—the gentle slope, soft underfoot, without sudden turnings, without milestones, without signposts."[8]

That's the way the prostitute works. She looks so attractive, and she painlessly seduces bit by bit until we find ourselves laughing at—or buying or saying or thinking or singing or doing—things we never would have before. Things that take us farther from God.

John knows that—before we realize it—the prostitute will take us farther than we want to go, keep us longer than we want to stay, and cost us more than we want to pay. So again, he throws back the curtain on evil. The culture which looks so attractive is actually a cheap, diseased streetwalker, and the devil is her pimp. Stay far away from her.

The dragon stalks us. Keep your eyes open.

Two Weapons

We have traced the marionette strings from godless government, false religion and hedonistic culture, back to Satan, their dark puppetmaster. We see now that the evil serpent breathes hot on our heels, his fiery flames threatening to catch us at any moment. But how can we possibly defeat this foe?

---

8. C. S. Lewis, *The Screwtape Letters* (San Francisco: HarperCollins, 1942) 61.

Revelation 12:11 tells us, "They overcame him by the blood of the Lamb and by the word of their testimony; they did not love their lives so much as to shrink from death.' We have two weapons: the first is to *claim the blood of Christ*. Christ defeated Satan on the cross, and we stand firmly in that victory!

The second is to *give your blood for Christ*. The martyrs singing in Revelation 12 were willing to die for love of Jesus. Whether we are called upon or not, we too must be willing to lay down our lives for Him. If we are, here is the truth the dragon cannot stand: his greatest power is killing us. But our greatest power is dying. If he kills us, then our testimony sealed in blood becomes unforgettable. Our greatest power always trumps his.

We have an enemy.

But if we stay faithful to Jesus, we win.

DISSCUSSION QUESTIONS
Chapter 9
See Evil Clearly

1. How often do you think about the reality of a spiritual Enemy? How does this awaremess (of lack thereof) affect your daily life?

2. In what ways are governments around the world oppressing believers? What can we do? How about our own American government?

3. What does our culture say about other religions? What does John say about them in Revelation 13? Do you know anyone in a false religion? How can we liberate such folk?

4. In what ways does our culture subtly (or not-so-subtly) draw us away from God? In entertainment? In our economy? Education? Social interaction? How can we resist?

CHAPTER TEN

AWAIT SALVATION EXPECTANTLY

Revelation 15-20

*"No form of Christian teaching has any future except
such as can keep steadily in view the reality of evil in the world
and go to meet the evil with a battle song of triumph."*
—Bishop Gustav Aulen—

The wrath of God is not a popular topic these days.

As Christians, we can be hesitant to speak of it, almost apologetic about it. We like to speak of God's grace, to sing "Jesus Loves Me" and to read books about the tender moments *When God Whispers Your Name*. (To be clear, I like all of these too.)

But I have never seen a book entitled *When God Yells Your Name*.

I have seen a congregation named The Church of God's Love. But I have never seen a building with a sign out front: The Church of God's Wrath. And I have never heard anyone sing, "Jesus shoves me, this I know."

Apparently our God never gets angry.

Maybe it's a reaction against a judgmental past, a time when pulpits thundered in storms of righteous anger but never broke forth in the sunlight of God's love. Maybe we see the Westboro Baptist Church picketing another funeral with hard, bitter faces and signs that read, "God Hates _____," and we want to be sure the world knows we're not like that. Maybe it's because so many in our broken culture come from abusive homes, and they desperately need a whole new concept for the word "father."

Not bad reasons. But in avoiding the truth of God's wrath, have we lost something?

A Wink In a Graveyard

A. J. Conyers tells of a time he visited historic Old Dorchester, South Carolina. A young historian employed by the parks department led the tour through the remains of the colonial city, his lecture re-creating the town in their imaginations as it might have been in the 1700's. After the marketplace and the colonial militia's parade grounds, he took them to old St. George's Anglican Church.

> We followed the historian down the grassy nave of the church, out into the churchyard and . . . we paused in a circle around a flat tombstone marking the grave of James Postell.
>
> The historian pulled a bit of paper out of his pocket. "Imagine," he said, "that we were there when James Postell was buried. As they lowered him into the ground, these are the words we would have heard from the 1768 *Book of Common Prayer*." In grave tones, and with expansive gestures of mock seriousness, he began: "Man that is born of woman, hath but a short time to live."
>
> The young man adjusted his wire-rimmed glasses, cleared his throat and went on: "In the midst of life we are in death: of whom may we seek for succor, but of Thee, O Lord, who for our sins are justly displeased?" Waving a hand out to the crowd and holding up the bit of paper in the other, he went on—thunder in his voice now: "Thou knowest, Lord, the secrets of our hearts; shut not thy merciful ears to our prayers; but spare us . . . suffer us not at our last hour for any pains of death to fall from thee."
>
> And then he winked.
>
> Why did he wink? It was because he knew very well that he shared a secret with us. James Postell—may he rest in peace—would never in this world understand, but we did. The secret that we shared is simply that we no longer take "otherworldly" sentiments seriously. Ideas about the brevity of life, the just judgment of present sinful life . . . all the fears that we could jeopardize an eternal state in the enjoyment of a temporal existence—all these topics are not a part of common polite, serious conversation.
>
> We understand the wink.[1]

A Theology Of the Nightly News

If the book of Revelation has taught us anything thus far, it's this: God's wrath is nothing to wink at. It is holy and terrible, full-blooded, just, fair, and completely unstoppable.

And that's a good thing. I want a God of wrath.

---

1. A. J. Conyers, Eclipse of Heaven, pp. 26-27.

That may sound strange . . . until you watch the nightly news. I hear of atrocities perpetrated around this sorry globe, and I shake my head in shock and disgust.

Stories of 10-year-old Cambodian girls sold into sex slavery. Stories of 13-year-old Congolese boys taken as child soldiers and brainwashed to kill. Stories of fathers and mothers working in offices on a September Tuesday morning when planes crash into their Towers with fiery destruction.

Murder, kidnapping, rape, blood diamond conflict, Chinese pastors thrown into prison, drug trafficking, Pakistani aid workers killed for distributing polio vaccines, Rwandan genocide, malnourished 10-year-old Courtney and six-year-old Logan in my town—left to fend for themselves for days because their mother was in the casino feeding her addiction.

When will it end? Who will stop the madness?

God will.

A God Who Is Coming To Save Us

Mark Buchanan tells the story of a man he knew whose younger brother has Down's Syndrome:

> One day when they were boys, some kids surrounded his brother and started calling him names, shoving him from one to the other. His round, thickset face grew taut with fear and bewilderment. The older brother, watching this, was at first afraid. But then he got angry, right good and angry. He wasn't physically big, and he was badly outnumbered; but in his anger he grew, and his strength multiplied. He waded in and whipped the whole lot of them.
>
> Stories like that resonate with something clean and deep and noble inside us. We know we are witnessing holy anger. We know, in the face of such things, that anything less than anger would be cowardice. It would be *pusillanimous,* a word whose literal meaning is "small spirit."[2]

Who wants a pusillanimous God? A God who sees the people he loves being brutalized by Satan, the bully of this world, and does nothing? No. I want a God who wades into the middle of our enemies and whips the lot of them.

I want a God of wrath.

---

2. Buchanan, *Holy Wild*, 100.

Revelation 15-20 shows us a God coming to judge with wrath. For those who commit atrocities on the nightly news — or who simply wink at the notion of a God and a Satan, a heaven and a hell — this is very bad news.

But for those who belong to Jesus, this is very good news. The persecuted believers of Asia Minor are surrounded by shoving tormenters, outnumbered and afraid, and they need someone to ride in to their rescue. These chapters tell us: he is coming to save. They show us three images of what that salvation looks like — a deliverance from slavery, a banquet at a wedding, and a victory in battle.

Salvation Is a Deliverance From Slavery

In Revelation 15 and 16, we come to the final series of seven judgments. As we've seen, the seven seals, trumpets and bowls all tell the same story — God's judgments leading up to the end of time. Each retelling of the story carried a different emphasis. If the first cycle's suffering purified the saints and the second cycle's suffering called sinners to repentance, then the final cycle's suffering simply unleashes full and final punishment on a rebel world (Rev 15:1).

In the seals, God set the dial on his wrath at 25%, affecting a fourth of the world, and in the trumpets, he turned the dial up to 33%. But with the seven bowls, his wrath is at a full 100% — all the world experiences his judgment.

These judgments, poured out from seven bowls held by seven angels, are called "the seven last plagues" (Rev 15:1). Indeed, they echo the plagues visited on Egypt when they held Israel in captivity — painful sores, water to blood, darkness, frogs hailstones. These chapters picture God's people as slaves again, oppressed and imprisoned in a pagan culture.

But God loves his people. So he releases his anger in order to release his people.

These plagues on unrepentant mankind are devastating, and some contemporary readers find such a scene hard to stomach. It does not square with their mental image of God, and they dismiss such portions of Scripture because "Jehovah does not think or behave like a social worker."[3] They believe God's love is incompatible with his wrath. But:

---

3. Peterson, Thunder, 162.

> It is hardly realistic to imagine a God of love who is not also a God of wrath. A mother whose child is in danger is more fearsome than a bear robbed of her cubs. A man whose lover is assaulted has a lethal zeal. It seems, therefore, that the greater the love, the greater the wrath. If that is true, then God's punishment of the wicked can be expected to match His love for the saints ... Some can't believe in a God of love who punishes His enemies. The Bible can't picture a God of love who doesn't![4]

So God unleashes his fury to save his people. His people, mind you, must be ready to be saved. Before the last plague struck Egypt, Moses told the Israelites to be ready to leave in the middle of the night — with staff in hand, sandals on their feet, and cloaks tucked into their belts ready to walk (Ex 12:11). Likewise, before the last plague in Revelation 16, John tells his readers that their moment of salvation will come suddenly and unexpectedly, so they must "stay awake" and "keep their clothes with them" (Rev 16:15). We must not be lulled into complacency and compromise with our captor culture. We must stay holy, prepared, constantly expectant.

After the saints are delivered from captivity, John pictures them standing by a sea (the one before God's throne) and singing "the song of Moses" — a victory ode like the one Israel sang after Pharaoh's army perished in the Red Sea (Rev 15:2-3).

In many ways, the story of Exodus is the story of the whole Bible. Right before the nation of Israel is established, God liberates his people from the bondage of Egypt. Fifteen hundred years later, right before the church is established, Jesus liberates his people from the bondage of sin through his death on the cross. Here in Revelation, right before the eternal kingdom of God is established, God liberates his people from the bondage of this world.

Our final salvation will be the ultimate exodus, and we can shout, "Free at last! Free at last! Thank God Almighty, we are free at last!"

Salvation Is a Banquet At a Wedding

I am a man and glad to be one. Maybe you've seen the list "Why It's Great To Be a Man," which includes things like:

- The garage is all yours.
- Phone conversations last 30 seconds.
- Bathroom lines are 80% shorter.

---

4. Moore, *Dragon*, 65.

- You can open all your own jars.
- You can watch a game in silence for hours without your buddy thinking, "He must be mad at me."

Ha! As a man, then, the metaphors in Revelation 17-19 are sometimes hard to wrap my head around, because here John gives us the choice to be one of two women. We can either be part of the Whore of Babylon or part of the Bride of Christ.

In Revelation 17:1, we again meet Satan's ally, the "great prostitute," symbolizing the corrupt culture of Rome. In Revelation 17 and 18, we read about her extravagant excesses, her voluptuous materialism, her seductive idolatries and wild orgies of persecution. Rome is a looker, but she's got a heart of ice.

With a prophet's eye, John looks ahead to the day of her destruction. This seemed ludicrous. Proud and confident, Rome called herself the "Eternal City." A saying commonly heard: "As long as the Coliseum stands, Rome shall stand. When the Coliseum falls, Rome will fall. When Rome falls, the world will fall." Rome seemed the very center of the world, and she could not conceive of a day when she would be laid low.

So Revelation 17 and 18 are "a literary triumph of imaginative power." When John wrote, the great pillared Roman Forum still dominated the city, the Coliseum still towered, the Circus Maximus still filled with 150,000 spectators, and the Temple of Jupiter with its gold-gilded roof still dazzled in the sun. Rome was very much alive, enjoying "undisputed sovereignty and undimmed prestige."[5]

No one saw the day, 300 years hence, when the barbarian hordes would pillage Rome. No one saw the day when the Empire would be only a distant memory, its great buildings rubble, a haunt for jackals.

No one, that is, except John. Here he describes Rome in "ruin" with the "smoke of her burning" blotting out the sky, all her merchants, and sailors and political allies weeping at her destruction (Rev 17:16;18:9). Distant though it may be, he knows her fate.

So John warns the believers: don't be seduced by this woman. Don't become a part of the Whore of Babylon. "Come out of her, my people, so that you will not share in her sins, so that you will not receive any of her plagues" (Rev 18:4).

---

5. Metzger, *Breaking*, 87.

In Greek mythology, Odysseus and his companions sail near the dangerous "island of sirens" and the seductive music woos them to the shore. To shut out the tempting songs, Odysseus stuffs his sailors' ears with cotton. Later, Orpheus and his seamen sail by the same enticing island. Orpheus protects his crew in a different manner: He takes out his lyre and *plays sweeter music* than the captivating island strains.

John knows the most effective way to resist temptation is to replace it with something better. So he shows us a more beautiful woman and a more glorious future. If we choose to be the faithful Bride of Christ, what awaits us? A great meal! As the Bride, we are invited to the wedding banquet of the Lamb (Rev 19:9). We will be given "fine linen, bright and clean" to wear (Rev 19:8).

Every year, I have in one my college classes at least one young lady engaged to be married at the end of the semester. They never have to tell me; I can spot them when they walk in the door. The young lady will be smiling as she floats in, her feet not even touching the ground. She's laughing, humming, singing . . . flunking all her classes . . . but she doesn't care. She's soon going to be with her groom! All is well.

Weddings are among the most joyful days we know as humans — love, beauty, food, family, dance — but this wedding will surpass them all. The Greatest Groom Ever, Jesus, is there! We will eat and rejoice and be glad forever (Rev 19:7).

And we will sing. Oh, will we sing! The only four uses of "Hallelujah" in the whole New Testament occur here, at the Lamb's wedding. Even the beautiful music of Orpheus will be a poor tune next to the glorious heart-soaring praise on that day when we get to be with our Groom! Our salvation will be the greatest wedding banquet you can imagine — only better — because we will be with the One whose love never ends. Hallelujah!

Salvation Is a Victory In Battle

Immediately after the banquet announcement, John says, "Behold, I saw heaven standing open." We expect to see a groom step through heaven's door, tux and tie, ready for a wedding (Rev 19:11). Instead out steps a warrior! He is a king arrayed for battle — fierce and awesome astride his white war charger, angel armies amassed at his back, a sharp sword brandished from his mouth, with a scepter like iron and eyes like fire.

This is our Champion.

One last reason "why it's great to be a guy": action movies. I love films like *Gladiator, Braveheart, Lord of the Rings,* even *The Avengers*—stories of a small embattled squadron of brave souls. Facing a powerful and evil enemy bent on destruction, the warriors find a noble captain worthy to lead them into battle. Their cause is righteous, but the odds are against them. Outnumbered and running out of time, how can they possibly win?

The movie builds, climbing, the air electric with tension, until finally our hero gathers his forces to charge the merciless foe. In the climactic battle, the momentum swings back and forth—ebb and flow, muscle and sweat, flash of sword and crash of shield—until terribly it seems the enemy is destined to win. Inexorably, the adversary bears down upon our champion, our hope all but gone as the enemy's victory seems certain.

But then, suddenly—one last great effort, an unexpected turn, a mighty swing, a catch of our breath, a lift of our heart—our hero has struck the enemy a fatal blow! Our company of soldiers is saved! The evil forces retreat in terror, the battle is over, and we are victorious!!

That is the story I expect to find here. All of Revelation, indeed of all history, has been leading to this moment—the climactic battle of history. The forces of good and evil have finally gathered. In Revelation 19 and 20, Jesus faces off against all our greatest enemies.

But here's the twist: there is no ebb and flow. There is no breathtaking last battle, no mortal struggle back and forth, no spectacle of warfare to keep us on the edge of our seats wondering who will prevail, no moment when we think our Champion might be overwhelmed. Yes, the enemies arrayed against our Hero are many, powerful, and horribly wicked.

But in an instant, Jesus just destroys them.

He's that powerful.

There is no long, drawn-out Armageddon conflict. It's the most lopsided battle in history.

He simply dispatches our enemies—one, two, three, done.

Our Final Three Enemies Destroyed

First, Jesus destroys the *demonic allies*. We have already seen the prostitute's demise, and now we see the first beast (godless government) and the second beast (false religion) thrown into the lake of fire. All the armies gathered with them are slaughtered, carrion for the scavenger birds who eat their bodies as "the great supper of God," a grim contrast to the wedding Banquet of the Lamb (Rev 19:17).

Second, Jesus destroys the *devil*. This happens after a "thousand years" during which Satan is bound and Jesus rules with the Christian faithful (Rev 20:1-6). Some Christians believe this "millennium" is a literal 365,000 days of Christ's reign (inaugurated at his return) as a global king on earth, Christian faithful physically resurrected at his side, all while Satan serves a physical 365,000 day sentence in the Abyss. At the end of the 1,000 years, Satan will be released, rally his troops for the great battle, and then is defeated by Christ, who at that time establishes the new heavens and the new earth.

Other Christians (including me) believe the "thousand years," like other numbers in Revelation is figurative, representing the long period of time between Christ's ascension and his return, the church's chapter in redemptive history. During this time, Christ reigns from his throne in heaven (as we've seen in Revelation 5) with the Christian faithful who've experienced spiritual resurrection in heaven, but not the resurrection of their physical bodies on earth.

Satan is bound spiritually during this church age by the preaching of the gospel, which hinders his "deceiving the nations" (Rev 20:3). As the gospel flourishes, Satanic strongholds diminish and the dominion of darkness falters. Right before Christ's Second Coming, Satan will be unbound, succeed in greater deception among the nations, and gather them for battle. Then in an instant, he will see them destroyed by fire from heaven as Jesus returns to inaugurate the new heavens and new earth.[6]

Either way, the devil takes an eternal swim in the lake of fire.

Either way, our enemy Satan is defeated.

Either way, Jesus wins.

Third and finally, Jesus destroys *death itself* (Rev 20:14). Death is the universal enemy. Some of us escape Satan's clutches, but nobody

---

6. These two primary views are called, respectively, the *pre-millenial* and the *amillenial* positions. Too often these have caused conflict among Christians, so let's practice humility whatever our understanding. If I'm wrong, I promise I will high five all my premillenial brothers and sisters when I get to heaven, congratulate them on being right, and then turn my full attention to what really matters—worshipping Jesus. As someone said about Christ's return, "I'm on the welcoming committee, not the planning committee."

escapes death. Throughout history, the statistics hold steady: 1 out of every 1 human being dies. But at the end of time, Jesus defeats our last enemy, throwing death into the lake of fire.

Can I say it again? I am glad we do not have a pusillanimous God.

I am thankful we do not have a God who is content to idly stand by as his people are savaged by our adversaries.

I am grateful we have a God who wades into the midst of our enemies and whips the lot of them.

Hear me: I want a God of wrath.

What a Savior

Until the moment I stand before the great white throne of judgment (Rev 20:11-15).

Then I am thankful for a God of mercy. For at that moment, no one will wink at the judgment of God. When God consults the book of our deeds, we will be judged by what we have done, and those who have disregarded God will be thrown into the lake of fire.

But if we have kept our faith in Christ, God will be merciful. If we have steadfastly worn the name of the Lamb, our name will be in the Lamb's book of life. Because Jesus bore God's wrath for our sins on the cross, we will be saved.

Praise God! Christ has delivered us from slavery. He has taken us as His Bride. He has defeated our every enemy.

Hallelujah! What a Savior!

DISSCUSSION QUESTIONS
Chapter 10
Await Salvation Expectantly

1. Do you think the American church has a healthy awareness of God's wrath? Why or why not? How would this awareness affect us? How is God's wrath an expression of love?

2. Of the three images of salvation discussed, which resonates with you the most? Why?

3. How does the picture of Jesus in Revelation 19 differ from his earthly ministry? From our culture's view of Christ?

4. How does the promise of evil's ultimate overthrow free us and focus us in our Christian life?

CHAPTER ELEVEN
DESIRE HEAVEN DEEPLY
Revelation 21-22

*"Heaven wheels above you, displaying to you her
eternal glories, and still your eyes are on the ground."*
—Dante Alighieri—

During his sermon on Revelation 21 and 22, the preacher exclaimed, "If you want to go to heaven, stand up!" The entire congregation stood—except one little boy in the front row. The preacher was perplexed. Looking over the pulpit, he said, "Son, do you mean to tell me that when you die, you don't want to go to heaven?"

"Oh, when I die, yes," said the boy. "I thought you were getting a group together to go right now!"

"Come, Lord Jesus ... Just Not Yet"

When I was younger, I didn't want to go to heaven very soon either.

To be honest, it didn't sound very exciting. As a kid, my mental picture of heaven went something like this: you die, go through the pearly gates, get your wings, halo, and a hymn book, and you join the heavenly choir. The choir director instructs us all to open our hymn books to hymn 1. "We are going to sing all four verses," he announces, "no skipping the third verse. We are going to sing our way straight though the hymn book, and when we get to the end, we'll start over again at the beginning." To me, heaven sounded like a church service gone really, really long.

Not very inspiring.

In Revelation 22:20, the apostle John teaches us to pray, "Come, Lord Jesus." But my prayer was, "Come, Lord Jesus ... just not yet." After all, I was young! I had so much in life left to do. There were books I hadn't read, mountains I hadn't climbed, whole seasons of *Gilligan's Island* I hadn't seen! I wanted to carve out great adventures, get married, have kids, travel the world and *then* maybe I'd be ready to go to heaven.

"Come, Lord Jesus ... just not yet."

The Eclipse Of Heaven

This world held more attraction for me than the next. Maybe I'm not the only one. As Christians, we are supposed to "set our hearts on things above" (Col 3:2). "Like the tug and heft of a huge unseen planet hovering nearby, the hope of heaven is meant to exert a gravitational pull" on our lives.[1]

However, to use A. J. Conyers phrase, we are living under "the eclipse of heaven." We live in a world that no longer believes in a transcendent reality, and even in the church "only a hint remains of the power heaven once exercised in the hearts of believers."[2] We are attached to this world, and when that happens, one of two problems occurs.

On the one hand, without a heaven, we can give in to the temptation to live for the here and now. That might be a life of hedonistic sin, but it might be something much more respectable. In church, we end up hearing sermons that are simply tips and techniques to have a fuller life now. Christianity becomes a way to better marriages, parenting, money management, and healthier habits. We hear very little about judgment, eternity, the gravity of our souls, and the urgency of evangelism. "Only heaven can prevent theology from becoming psychology."[3]

On the other hand, without a heaven, we might just give in to hopelessness. Over the last decade, suicide among middle-aged Americans rose almost 30%. P. T. Forsyth said, "If within us we find nothing over us, we succumb to what is around us." If the trials of life lack any "redemptive denouement" (a fancy theological term for "good ending to the story"), why even try to endure?

A Robust Eschatological Imagination

These twin problems could easily affect the churches of Asia Minor unless they cultivate a robust eschatological imagination (another fancy theological term for a "healthy mental picture of heaven").

So John helps them do exactly that. In Revelation 21-22, John paints amazing pictures of heaven. He exercises a "robust eschatological imagination," and the images he projects onto our mental screens grab our attention like a summer blockbuster in a darkened theater.

---

1. Buchanan, *Things Unseen*, 24.
2. A. J. Conyers, *The Eclipse of Heaven* (Downer's Grove: IVP, 1992) 11.
3. *Ibid.*, 193.

By the way, C. S. Lewis gives us a wise reminder about the imagery here:

> There is no need to be worried by facetious people who try to make the Christian hope of "Heaven" ridiculous by saying they do not want "to spend eternity playing harps." The answer to such people is that if they cannot understand books written for grown-ups, they should not talk about them. All the scriptural imagery (harps, crowns, gold, etc.) is, of course, a merely symbolical attempt to express the inexpressible.
>
> Musical instruments are mentioned because for many people (not all) music is the thing known in the present life which most strongly suggests ecstasy and infinity. Crowns are mentioned to suggest the fact that those who are united with God in eternity share His splendor and power and joy. Gold is mentioned to suggest the timelessness of Heaven (gold does not rust) and the preciousness of it. People who take these symbols literally might as well think that when Christ told us to be like doves, He meant that we were to lay eggs.[4]

When I read those paragraphs as a Bible college freshman, I suddenly realized that my previous mental images of heaven were inadequate—that I needed to re-read Revelation 21-22 with a richer imagination. Perhaps then my heart would begin to long deeply for heaven.

Maybe I would learn to pray simply, "Come, Lord Jesus."

Along with John's readers, I found heaven described with three primary images: a *paradise*, a *city* and a *temple*.

Heaven Is Described As a Paradise

Revelation 21-22 reverberates with language from Genesis 1-2. The tree of life, no pain, no death, no curse—these are all echoes of Eden. This is Paradise restored, the world as God originally intended.

Notice that we do not go to heaven. Heaven comes to us. "The Holy City, the new Jerusalem" comes down out of heaven and settles on a brand, new incarnation of planet earth. Heaven is a profoundly physical place. Contrary to popular opinion, heaven is not a white, fuzzy, soft-focus netherworld, and we will not be disembodied souls floating around like Casper the Friendly Ghost on cloud nine. We will live in a new heaven and a new *earth* (21:1), a real physical world.

---

4. C. S. Lewis, *Mere Christianity* (New York: Macmillan, 1943) 120-121.

When my son Luke was six, we stood in the backyard preparing to bury his goldfish. (Unfortunately, it was the third one we had failed to keep alive.) Goldie III was in a matchbox coffin, soon to join his predecessors in our tiny goldfish graveyard. Luke looked up and asked quietly, "Dad, will there be animals in heaven?"

I had to stop for a moment to think, and before I could answer, suddenly Luke's face brightened, "Oh wait, dad, I already know the answer. I remember the story in the Bible when Elijah went to heaven, and the chariot of fire came to get him. It was pulled by horses of fire! So I guess there *are* animals in heaven. Whew, I'm glad! Thanks for the help, dad."

I said, "You're welcome, son."

Then I thought, "Hey, that's pretty good. I'm going to write that down and use that sometime." Because Luke is right. Someday we will live in a new earth with animals and rivers and mountains and trees. Paradise (a Persian word for "garden") will be a place of breathtaking beauty.

No More . . .

This new earth will not be under the curse (Rev 22:3). Currently, along with bright red tulips and galloping horses and glory-painted sunsets, we also have mosquitoes, mudslides, weeds, and drought. But in the paradise to come, there will be no more wildfires, tsunami, or EF-5 tornadoes. Four months ago, my wife was diagnosed with endometrial stromal sarcoma. Our life since has been doctors and hospitals, medicines and surgeries, worries and bills.

In the new world, there will be no cancer.

We will have new bodies (1 Cor 15:35ff), and with no curse, the effects of time will be no more. Time eats at all things. With the passing days, cars rust, fruit rots, and our bodies break down. (If you're over 40, can I get a witness?)

Time is not our friend, and the second law of thermodynamics — the universe is running down — gets us all. My grandpa was a farmer and could work from sunup to sundown, a strong and strapping man in his day. But as the years went by, he moved more slowly. His hearing and eyesight dimmed, his back weakened, his body suffered the effects of a corrupted world.

But what if we lived in a world where the effects of time were gone? A comedian once imagined what life would look like if time worked backward:

> I think the life cycle is all backward. You should die first, get that out of the way. Then you live twenty years in an old-age home where you wake up feeling better each day. Then you get kicked out when you're too young. You go collect your pension and get a gold watch on your first day at work. You work forty years until you're young enough to enjoy your retirement. You go to college and have a great time with your friends until you're ready for high school. You go to grade school; you become a little kid; you play. You have no responsibilities. You become a little baby; you go back into the womb; you spend your last nine months floating peacefully, and you finish up as a gleam in somebody's eye.[5]

When we read that, we laugh. But "what if?" If there is time in eternity, what if it somehow works backwards? Every day is fresher and brighter than the one before. The second law of thermodynamics is suddenly reversed, and everything gets better with time. Fruit gets sweeter, clothes get newer, floors get cleaner. Every morning in the new heavens and new earth, my grandpa will wake up to go work in the fields he loved, and he will feel stronger and healthier and younger than the day before.

There will be no death, no empty chairs at the dinner table, no child-sized caskets, no lonely widows. Heaven will be this beautiful green and blue planet we inhabit—finally restored the way God intended.

"Come, Lord Jesus."

Heaven Is Described As a City

Heaven is also described as a city—"the new Jerusalem" (Rev 21:2).

As an Iowa country kid who grew up surrounded by corn, "city" has not always been a warm word for me. It brought to mind words like noisy, crowded, dirty, dangerous, crime, pollution. I like green space and open sky. Why would heaven be a city?

In the movie *Field of Dreams*, the ballplayers from days gone by slowly step out of the cornfields onto the baseball diamond. One of them looks around in amazement and asks, "Is this heaven?" "No," comes the answer. "It's Iowa."

---

5. Quoted in Mike Yaconelli, *Dangerous Wonder*

That might be my favorite movie line of all time.

That's what heaven's supposed to look like — green pastures. Why a city? If you read Revelation 21 carefully, the city is a metaphor. Cities are where people congregate and live together. A city is a symbol of community, and this particular city symbolizes the community of God. The Holy City comes down from heaven "prepared as a bride beautifully dressed for her husband" (Rev 21:2). We recognize that language — the bride is the Church.

So this city represents the people of God. In fact, the twelve gates bear the names of Israel's twelve tribes — God's Old Testament people. The twelve foundations bear the names of the Church's twelve apostles — God's New Testament people.

Heaven is where we live forever in the community of believers.

As we tour the city, we notice the beauty — gold and precious stones and pearls, perfectly symmetrical proportions. The picture is simply of a city beautiful and perfect. Here's the point: we, the people of God, will finally be made beautiful and perfect. The Bride will be "a radiant church, without stain or wrinkle or any other blemish, but holy and blameless" (Eph 5:27).

Sin will be no more (Rev 21:8).

Becoming More Human Than You've Ever Been

So not only will Nature be redeemed, but my own personal sin nature will also be redeemed. I know my own sin. Steve Brown, a preacher in Florida, tells about a woman who came up to him after a sermon and said, "You know, I've heard a lot of preachers say that they are sinners. But you're the first one I ever believed!"

You can believe me when I say I'm a sinner. My autobiography reads like Paul's in Romans 7:19, "For what I do is not the good I want to do; no, the evil I do not want to do — this I keep on doing." Some mornings, I look in the mirror and am disappointed in what I see.

But in the new world, I will be redeemed — free from all contaminants and lesser things.

C. S. Lewis said, "To enter heaven is to become more human than you ever succeeded in being on earth," and there I will be the Matt Proctor that God always intended me to be. I will be my best self forever.

You will be your best self forever, and our relationships will no longer bear the effects of sin—no anger, guilt or abuse; no bitterness, gossip or betrayal; no lying, pride or shame. I love one author's imaginative description of this redeemed community:

> In a world [redeemed from sin], all marriages would be healthy and all children would be safe. Those who have too much would give to those who have too little. Israeli and Palestinian children would play together on the West Bank; their parents would build homes for one another. In offices and corporate boardrooms, executives will secretly scheme to help their colleagues succeed; they would compliment them behind their backs. Tabloids would be filled with accounts of courage and moral beauty. Talk shows would feature mothers and daughters who love each other deeply, wives who give birth to their husbands' children, and men who secretly enjoy dressing as men.
>
> Disagreements would be settled with grace and civility. There would still be lawyers, perhaps, but they would have really useful jobs, like delivering pizza, which would be non-fat and low in cholesterol. Doors would have no locks; cars would have no alarms. Schools would no longer need police presence or even hall monitors; students and teachers and janitors would honor and value one another's work. At recess, every kid would get picked for a team.
>
> Churches would never split.
>
> People would be neither bored or hurried. No father would ever again say, "I'm too busy" to a disappointed child. Divorce courts and battered-women shelters would be turned into community recreation centers. Every time one human being touched another, it would be to express encouragement, affection and delight.
>
> No one would be lonely or afraid. People of different races would join hands; they would honor and be enriched by their differences and be united in their common humanity.
>
> And in the center of the entire community will be its magnificent architect and most glorious resident: God Himself.[6]

I'm a country kid from Iowa, but that's a city I want to live in. "Come, Lord Jesus."

Heaven Is Described As a Temple

Besides a paradise and a city, John uses the image of a temple to describe heaven.

You might have missed it. After all, the apostle says, "I did not see a temple in the city" (Rev 21:22). But John gave us a clue. He records for us the dimensions of the city: 12,000 stadia (about 1,400 miles) long

6. Ortberg, *Everybody's Normal*, 19-20.

and high and wide. In other words, the city is a perfect cube . . . and there is only one other perfect cube described in all of Scripture.

The Holy of Holies in Israel's Temple.

The Holy of Holies was the Temple's innermost room where God himself dwelt between the cherubim on the Ark of the Covenant. The Holy of Holies had extremely limited access—only the High Priest could go in, and even he could only do so one day a year. God was pretty hard to get to back then.

But not in heaven.

In heaven, the city itself is the Holy of Holies, and we constantly live in the presence of God. That's the promise of Revelation 21:3, "Now the dwelling of God is with men, and he will live with them." The presence of God is what makes heaven, heaven. Finally, the veil that has separated us from God will been torn, and we will have full and free access to the One we love. We will enjoy the benefits of heaven, but the beauty of heaven is seeing God.

Coming Down the Aisle

William Dyke was a witty and handsome young man. Though struck blind at the age of ten, he did not allow his handicap to keep him from living life to the fullest. While attending graduate school in England, William met the daughter of a British admiral, won her heart, and proposed. She happily accepted.

Before agreeing to give his daughter's hand in marriage, however, the admiral insisted that William undergo a potentially dangerous surgery to restore his sight. William agreed, but he too had a condition. He insisted that, after the surgery, the gauze remain on his eyes until the moment of the wedding. He wanted his bride's face to be the first thing he saw with his new sight.

The surgery was completed, and the wedding day came. William's father stood next to his son at the front of the church, and the bride's father began to lead her down the aisle. As she walked, William's father began to unwind the gauze from his eyes. No one knew if the operation had been successful.

Just as William's bride arrived before him at the altar, the last strand of gauze was pulled away. He stood face-to-face with his beloved, and the entire congregation waited, breathless, wondering if William could actually see.

Finally William spoke, words those in attendance never forgot: "You are more beautiful than I ever imagined."

A day is coming when that story will be ours. The roles will be reversed, for we are the Bride who now can only see our Groom as "through a glass darkly, but then face to face" (1 Cor 13:12). In heaven, the Holy of Holies, the veil will be removed, and we will look fully into the face of the One we love.

He will be more beautiful than we ever imagined.

"Come, Lord Jesus."

DISSCUSSION QUESTIONS
Chapter 11
Desire Heaven Deeply

1. What's your mental image of heaven? Eternal retirement village? Long church service? How does our view of heaven affect our life on a daily basis?

2. What effects of a fallen creation have you personally experienced? What do you think you will enjoy the most about a renewed planet Earth?

3. Sin mars our human relationships. How have you felt the pain of sine's relational effects? On author imagined a redeemed community. What do you think it might include?

4. In heave we get to see God. If you could ask God one question when you get there, what would it be? What quality of God do you think you'll enjoy when you meet Him?

CHAPTER TWELVE

HOPING FOR A HAPPY MEAL

A Final Reflection on Revelation

"I have come home at last! This is my real country! I belong here. This is the land I have been looking for all my life, though I never knew it till now. The reason why we loved the old Narnia is that it sometimes looked a little like this. Come further up, come further in!"
—Jewel the Unicorn in C. S. Lewis' *The Last Battle*—

I love McDonald's.

Every Saturday morning growing up, my dad would take me (or one of my brothers) to McDonald's for breakfast, so I have warm memories of the Golden Arches. When Katie and I went on our very first date, I took her out for a movie and ice cream—at McDonald's. I wanted to share the goodness.

On the one-year anniversary of that occasion, I took Katie back to that same McDonald's. When she ordered, the McDonald's guy at the register brought out from under the counter a great big vase of red roses. (They were from me, not the McDonald's guy.) Then I took her back to the booth where we'd had our first date, got down on my knee, and I proposed to my wife . . . at McDonalds.

Clearly I am a hopeless romantic.

So you can understand why, early in life, my kids developed a love for McDonald's, and I quickly learned that my children always wanted to order the same thing. Every trip to McDonald's , they wanted the kid's package that someone, in a moment of marketing genius, called a Happy Meal. Because you are not just buying a burger, fries, drink and a fifty-cent toy. Oh no. You are buying *happiness*.

John Ortberg writes about Happy Meals:

> You know McDonald's inflates the price far beyond the value of the toy. I try to buy the kids off sometimes. I tell them just to order food off the dollar menu, and I'll give them some quarters to buy a toy on their own. But no, the cry goes up, "I want a Happy Meal!" All over the restaurant, people crane their necks to look at the tight-fisted, penny-pinching cheapskate of a parent who would deny a child the meal of great joy. So I buy each child his own, and they're happy — at least for a minute and 30 seconds.
>
> The problem with Happy Meals is that the Happy always wears off.[1]

The Problem With Happy Meals

That's true. No child discovered lasting happiness in a kids' meal at McDonald's. When the excitement wears off, they need a new fix. You would think after a while that kids would catch on, but they don't. They keep buying them, and they keep not working.

The problem with Happy Meals is that the "Happy" always wears off.

Ortberg concludes, "Of course, only a child would be so naïve. Only a child could be foolish enough to believe that a change in circumstance could bring lasting contentment. Or maybe not. Maybe when you get older, you don't necessarily get any smarter; your Happy Meals just get more expensive."[2]

Let's be honest: as part of the human race, we all feel the hunger. We all have a vague sense of disappointment, of discontentment, a nagging feeling that something is missing. We try to feed it with all sorts of things: work, hobbies, family, achievement, cars, relationships, food, sex, money. The Happy Meals are all different, but the hunger is universal. We're all looking for something.

Here's the rub: even when we find what we're looking for, it doesn't fully satisfy. We all feel disappointment in life when things go wrong — the pipes burst, the marriage breaks up, cancer strikes, the job promotion falls through. But I'm talking about disappointment when things go right. The marriage is good, you get the job, the house remodeling looks great, and yet somewhere in the early morning hours, as you lie awake in the dark, you are haunted by the feeling that it isn't quite enough.

---

1. John Ortberg, "Happy Meal Spirituality" *Christianity Today* (May 17, 1993) 38.
2. John Ortberg, *Love Beyond Reason* (Grand Rapids: Zondervan, 1998) 92-93.

When Hall of Fame quarterback Troy Aikman won his first Super Bowl with the Dallas Cowboys, he did not go with his teammates to celebrate. Instead he ordered a beer from room service and sat alone in his hotel room. He told a reporter, "I kept thinking back to when I was a teenager—how I thought life's problems would be solved when I turned 16 and got a car. But they weren't. Now here I was at the top of professional football, and I found myself thinking the same thing, 'Is this all there is? Now what?'"

Alexander the Great conquered the known world, and when he found there were no more nations to conquer, he sat down and wept. Christian author Mark Buchanan remembers when he held in his hand his first published book—representing 20 years of dreaming and eight years of writing. After all the prayers, hopes, and knocking on publishers' doors, it was supposed to be a glorious moment. But Mark writes, "It wasn't enough. It didn't answer all my longings or quell all my insecurities. It didn't fulfill me."[3]

The problem with Happy Meals is that the "Happy" always wears off.

This World Is Overrated

If you live long enough, you discover: this whole world is overrated. It is rigged for disappointment. It gives us stones for bread. When we get what we want, it's never quite enough. Satisfaction never lasts, and even our joys are tinged with sadness. In Ecclesiastes, King Solomon—the man who literally had it all—wrote, "Meaningless! Meaningless! Everything is meaningless. Nothing was gained. It is all a chasing after the wind."

Solomon knew better than anyone: the Happy always wears off.

So the question is, "What will satisfy the hunger?"

C. S. Lewis once wrote:

> Creatures are not born with desires unless satisfaction for those desires exists. A baby feels hunger: well, there is such a thing as food. A duckling wants to swim: well, there is such a thing as water . . . If I find in myself a desire which no experience in this world can satisfy, the most probable explanation is that I was made for another world . . . Earthly pleasures were never meant to satisfy it, but only to arouse it, to suggest the real thing."[4]

3. Buchanan, *Things Unseen*, 44.
4. Lewis, *Mere Christianity*, 119.

This world isn't meant to satisfy that hunger. It's meant to whet our appetite. The dissatisfaction that we feel with this world "is not so much a design flaw as a *designed* flaw."[5] God has wired discontentment into the system so that we would not mistake this world for our home—so that we would not lose our hunger for something deeper and stronger and truer. Solomon himself named it in Ecclesiastes: "God has set *eternity* in the hearts of men" (Ecc 3:11).

What we hunger for is heaven.

Stirring the Hunger For Heaven

The seven churches of Asia Minor needed their hunger for heaven stirred.

That's why the book of Revelation was written. A few of the churches, conforming to the society around them, were chasing money and sex and the tokens of cultural respectability. They needed a reminder that the things of this world will never truly satisfy. John knew that, after every Happy Meal, they would wake up the next day hungry again.

They needed their sights set on things above, a reminder that all the good things of this world are simply "rumors of another world." Every pleasure of this life is a preview of coming attractions, but it is not the Main Event. Every good gift is an echo, but not the Voice. Every earthly satisfaction is only a clue pointing to something greater, not the Treasure itself. So John writes to turn their attention from these shadowlands below to the sunlit lands above.

Of course, some of these churches had not compromised, and therefore were undergoing grave persecution—hardship upon hardship. When we experience great pain, it can be easy to forget everything else. If a toothache can "eliminate awareness of health in every other part of the body," think of how such constant harsh mistreatment could have blotted out everything else for these hurting believers.[6] In the presence of such oppressive darkness, the hope of heaven may have seemed quite dim.

---

5. Buchanan, *Things Unseen*, 53.
6. Peterson, *Thunder*, 73.

Teaching Us To Hope

So John writes to brighten their hope, to rekindle their expectation, to stir their hunger for heaven. He knew that hopeful anticipation was essential to their survival.

Since a diving accident left her a quadriplegic as a teen, Joni Eareckson Tada has been living in a wheelchair for over 45 years. She says, "The art of living with suffering is the art of readjusting your expectations in the here and now. We ask less of this life because we know full well that more is coming in the next."

That is what Revelation does: it readjusts our expectation. We lower our expectations of this life—Revelation tells us we'll probably experience more hardships than Happy Meals. But we raise our expectations of the next life—Revelation tells us that a day is coming when we'll be outrageously triumphant and eternally blessed.

Revelation keeps reminding us: *if we'll just stay faithful in the middle of the story, we'll be victorious in the end.*

How do we stay faithful? Our journey through Revelation has taught us to see Christ in all his power, to stay connected to our imperfect church, to lose ourselves in worship, to trust patiently in the midst of suffering, to witness courageously, see past evil's disguises, keep ourselves pure and wait expectantly for God's perfect salvation.

But most of all, Revelation has taught us to hope. It has taught us to fix our hearts on heaven. God's eternal kingdom—that is what we've always been looking for. "Heaven is the ache in our bones, the splinter in our heart."[7] Heaven is our deepest instinct. Heaven is our heart's true home.

One Final Picture

Revelation is a book of metaphors meant to fire your imagination. So can I close this little book with my kindergarten-crayon attempt to do the same? I'll leave you with a picture.

The picture hangs in our bedroom. It's a photograph of a place that is my wife's heart.

My wife comes from a little village of a hundred people called Irwin, Missouri, and the large photograph on our bedroom wall is of the farm where she grew up. If you left our house in Joplin and drove

---

7. Buchanan, *Things Unseen*, 29.

about 45 minutes north on Highway 71, you'd see off to your right Highway C. Turn east on Highway C, and in about a half mile, you'll go over some railroads tracks. Off to your left, you'll see a big white hay barn. Turn in at the driveway right past the hay barn, and you've arrived at Bunton Farms.

My wife comes from a big farming clan—she's the youngest of five kids—and that farm has been in her family for over 60 years. Her dad Don farmed it, her older brothers (Marty, Mike and Matt) have farmed it, and the grandsons are big enough these days to do a fair share of the work as well.

The picture in our bedroom is an aerial shot of the homestead, taken the summer that Katie was 14 years old, and in the corner of the photograph is a handwritten note from Katie's mother Ruth. Katie's mama—we call her Granny—has been faithfully keeping a daily journal all her life, and the note records what was happening the day the photo was taken. It reads:

AUGUST 10, 1983

It's not ART, but it's HOME to Bunton Farms, Inc., Irwin, MO (and to the Irwin 4-H club). The camera didn't catch (but Mom's journal shows):

Katie bringing the rakes in at the end of haying

Mike and Matt taking a bale wagon load to a hay customer

Marty on a 3-wheeler checking irrigation

Bunton Reunion company staying overnight (and Don actually inside visiting)

Ruth picking blackberries beyond the oaks

AND IT WAS HOT THAT DAY!

When I look at that picture, I see the farmhouse and could not begin to count the number of family dinners we've eaten underneath that roof. I see the front yard and think of all the Easter egg hunts the grandkids have laughed through there. I see the gravel driveway in front of the barn, and I can hear all the arguments Katie's brothers have had out there. (They're always friends by the end of the day.)

When my wife sees that picture, there are more memories than you could shake a stick at. That farm is my wife Katie's favorite place in the world, and her roots go so deep on that piece of land that her veins run with Barton County dirt.

Sometimes on a summer Saturday morning, our family hops in the car, drives 45 minutes north on Highway 71 and then heads east on Highway C. Right after the railroad tracks, we pull into the driveway just past the white hay barn, and we can already see Granny coming out the front door, smiling, to greet us. I will tell you: at that moment, my wife's heart lets out a deep sigh of belonging.

It's not art, but it's home.

A Rumor Of Heaven

So we all pile out of the car for a day on the farm. Katie's brothers and their kids are working — laying pipe, fixing fence, spraying crops, digging ponds. Hot work, hard work. We jump in and try to help — driving pickups, changing tires. There's satisfaction in the work, but everybody's looking forward to 7:00 p.m. Sometime around then, we all head back to Granny's house.

Katie's mom is the family matriarch, and her kitchen table is the family sanctuary, where we all congregate for meetings, formal and informal. When we arrive at Granny's, she's cooking supper: mashed potatoes and gravy, her famous biscuits, maybe some apple pie. (I love apple pie!) The table is loaded.

Out the back door, on the gravel driveway, Grandpa Don is frying up some fish. While we're waiting on supper, my job is (and always has been) to get a baseball game started. We pull out the bat and ball, still wearing our work clothes, and out in the front yard, I'm all-time pitcher. My kids play with cousins, aunts, uncles — Grandpa himself comes out when the fish are done frying. We have four generations out there in the fading summer sunlight, whooping and hollering and hitting the ball.

Then Granny calls us in for supper. We wash up and dig in, then back for seconds, then some ice cream and a piece of apple pie, and then we're full.

It's dark outside now, and we push back a bit from the table, sitting, talking, laughing, kids running around our feet. Stories are told, funny and serious. Then before everyone leaves, Granny calls one of the granddaughters to the piano — she's taking piano lessons, you know — and she says, "It's time for a song." There, still around the table, we sing *Now Thank We All Our God*.

After the song ends, there is a moment, a beat, a fleeting still silence as the last notes fade, when we all remain exactly where we are, reflecting, faint smiles on all the faces, soaking in the life we've just shared, secure in a family's love.

That memory is one of the purest moments I know.

For a brief window of time, all things are as they are supposed to be, and the joy of that moment aches in my chest.

That moment is a rumor of heaven.

The Meal Of Great Joy

The message of Revelation is this: a day is coming when our work will be done. Our long and difficult labor in the fields will cease. The last trumpet will sound, the sun will sink in the west, time shall be no more, and as we pull in the driveway of the Celestial City, our souls will let out a deep sigh of belonging.

We will be home.

It will be Jesus himself coming out the front door to greet us, smiling, "Well done, good and faithful servant." And he will invite us in for a meal, the wedding banquet of the Lamb, with people gathered round from every tongue and tribe and nation. On that table will be the richest of fare, delights unending — an apple pie so big that an angel will have to draw his sword to cut the pieces! We will sit and eat and talk with brothers and sisters that we have never met and those that we have loved dearly.

When we have finished eating, we will push back from the table and tell our stories, laughter filling the great hall. Then at some moment, all eyes will turn, and at the far end of the table, we will see our King seated on his throne, and we will hear him say, "It is time for a song."

At that great meal, he will come and sing to us. Haunting, healing, holy music — he will sing until our wounded hearts are bound up and made whole, sing until our hungry souls are filled, sing until the joy pierces us like a sword. Our delight will overflow until it mingles with the very river of God.

We shall weep tears of joy, and he will come and wipe them from our eyes and whisper, "Peace, my child. Rest and drink and eat. Be satisfied forever. Laugh and talk and work and learn and enjoy me.

For all that is sad and evil has become untrue, and all that is good has become true. We are together now, and we will be together forever. All shall be well, and all shall be well, and all manner of things shall be well."

We will be secure in his love, and that moment—that moment will never end.

That, my friend, will be the meal of great joy.

That will be the Happiest Meal of all.

Stay faithful to Jesus.

DISSCUSSION QUESTIONS
Chapter 12
Hoping For A Happy Meal

1. Have you chased after a particular "Happy Meal" in your life that you thought would satisfy? How did that turn out?

2. "The art of living with suffering is the art of readjusting your expectations in the here and now." What expectations do you need readjusted? How would this change the way you live?

3. An evening at the tabel with family provides a hint of heaven. If the good gifts of this world ar "rumors of another world," what things in your life point you upward?"

4. On a scale of 1-10, how strong is your hope? What can you do to cultivate the kind of hope that will help you endure with Jesus?